TRUST and OBEY

A Practical Commentary on

FIRST PETER

JAY E. ADAMS

BAKER BOOK HOUSE
Grand Rapids, Michigan

To Heather . . .

Keep on serving Christ
cheerfully, all your days!

Copyright 1979 by
Baker Book House Company
ISBN: 0-8010-0145-5

Printed in the United States of America

Contents

Foreword

I Peter is a neglected book. Because of its pertinence to our times, those that may soon come upon us and the entire counseling enterprise, I have done this study.

This is not a critical commentary; there are enough of those already. This is a practical commentary that attempts to consider the book in the light of how it may be preached, used in daily life and employed in counseling. Christians, hopefully, will find it helpful in their struggles with suffering. Expositions are followed by sermon sketches. Each section constitutes a preaching portion.

My prayer is that Christians will be helped directly and indirectly to follow God's instructions for facing trials and tribulations summed up in the words TRUST AND OBEY.

JAY ADAMS
The Millhouse
Juliette, GA
1978

The text used throughout is from *The New Testament in Everyday English*, by Jay Adams.

CHAPTER ONE

Section One

Peter, an apostle of Jesus Christ, to those who are scattered about as refugees in Pontus, Galatia, Cappadocia, Asia and Bithynia (I Pet. 1:1).

Peter identifies himself to his readers as **an apostle of Jesus Christ.** Simon, whose name Jesus changed to **Peter** (which means Rock[1]) had been reinstated as **an apostle** by the risen Lord and reappointed to the pastoral (shepherdly) work of caring for God's flock (John 21:1-19). Presumably, the name **Peter** was used predominantly in the church, and the apostle (when acting as such) himself used it (but see Galatians 1:9, 11; the use of Peter in vss. 7, 8, 9, followed by a change to Cephas, may indicate that, in Paul's opinion, Peter had not been acting in an apostolic manner on the occasion to which he refers).

An apostle[2] was one "sent forth" or "sent off" on a mission. It signified both his work and its representative character. The Greek word *apostello,* "to send off," and the Latin word *mitto,* from which our modern term "missionary" comes, are exact equivalents. The twelve apostles were the first missionaries in the church. Others, like

---

1. Other views, such as distinguishing between *Petros* and *Petra,* do not satisfy. The change of name (John 1:42) indicates the change that Jesus intended to effect in the man. For comments on this, see my *Competent to Counsel.* Christ made Peter the Rock (Matt. 16:18) in the sense that he was privileged to *found* the church; it was Peter who first proclaimed the gospel to the Jews (Acts 2) and to the Gentiles (Acts 10). At these two "pentecosts" he used the keys to the church and unlocked the doors for both Jew and Gentile. There is nothing about apostolic succession or about the office of pope in the New Testament.

2. Jesus Himself designated the twelve as apostles (Luke 6:13); from the beginning He chose them for this ministry (Mark 3:14; the verb "send forth" is the word from which the noun "apostle" comes).

3

our missionaries today, also bore the title (cf. Phil. 2:25, where Epaphroditus is called the "apostle" of the Philippian church to Paul. Epaphroditus had been "sent off" to minister to Paul as their representative. He ministered in their name. So too the twelve served in Christ's name). But the Twelve (a designation used to distinguish them as a separate group—Mark 6:7; Luke 8:1; 9:1, etc.) were Christ's representatives, directly responsible to Him, to whom were given special powers to authenticate and identify them as such (II Cor. 12:12; Acts 14:3; Heb. 2:3, 4). The power to exercise and to dispense miraculous gifts attested to the divine authority of both the messenger and his message. Like Epaphroditus, modern missionaries derive their authority from Christ indirectly through His church as its representatives. It is not the missionaries alone who engage in missionary work but, through them, the whole church (III John 8).

In this letter, Peter's concerns are distinctively pastoral. This concern grew from trials that those flocks over which he had particular supervision were facing. Persecution, both present and imminent, is the problem that dominates all else. The thematic question of the letter is: "How should a Christian face persecution?" And the answer, best summed up in 4:19, is "Trust and obey." The theme makes this an important letter for counseling purposes as well as for preaching.

Peter takes up his pen to warn, to instruct, to remind (a favorite thought and theme of his; he had known the consequences of forgetting in his earlier relationships with Jesus) and to encourage (the whole first chapter rings with various notes of encouragement).

Jewish Christians, **scattered** (a technical term—"scattering" or "sowing"—first used of Jews of the dispersion, who had been spread abroad about the Mediterranean world like seed broadcast by a sower. Here, the concept is in view, but narrowed to include Jewish *Christians*[3] now living) **as refugees in Pontus, Galatia, Cappadocia, Asia and Bithynia.**

The fact that Peter describes his readers as **refugees scattered**

---

3. Peter was chosen to be the apostle to the Jews (cf. Gal. 2:7, 8). Thus, in harmony with that divine choice, Peter was supervising the affairs of the

4

about is an indication that the persecution had already caused much hardship. The same verb ("to sow or scatter") is used to describe the **scattering** of the early church from Jerusalem under the persecution of Saul (who later became Paul the apostle; cf. Acts 8:1, 4). According to Acts 8:4, that **scattering** had resulted in a great spread of the gospel. But since, at that time, the **scattering** had driven them no farther than to Judea and Samaria, we can suppose that Peter (while possibly also having this event in mind) refers to subsequent **scatterings** under persecution.

At any rate, the word **refugees** clearly strikes the note of suffering loss and deprivation, which in an introductory sermon on the book of I Peter ought to be sounded at the outset. Everything that follows—including the encouragements and assurances (not to speak of the ever-recurring emphasis upon personal responsibility in suffering)—ought to be preached in the context of suffering. Otherwise, much of the meaning (and hence the power) of the book and of individual passages will be lost. Every sermon from I Peter—in one way or another—ought to be related to the theme of suffering (persecution) for Christ's sake. Here, by citing recent examples of the suffering of **refugees** or (in the event that these are not available) the hardships of **refugees** from Hungary, Cuba, Vietnam and other Indo-Chinese countries may help to make the point. Differences, however, also may be noted; these Christians (in addition to those outrages and those trials commonly inflicted upon **refugees** in general) had undergone many afflictions *for Christ's sake*. Questions about their faith—such as, "Why has the Lord allowed these things to happen?"—added to their problems. And, for those who had no such questions, the very difficult question of *how* one should respond to the indignities and agonies of persecution were uppermost. All of these burning issues lie behind the inspired words Peter has written. But the Spirit of God wrote not only for Peter's time; what He says pertains equally to Christians of every age, including our day. In every Bible-believing congregation there are Christians facing some

---

Jewish churches. There are indications in the letter that some Gentiles were included too.

5

form of persecution and suffering with similar questions on their lips. Vital preaching of the principles, practices and promises of this book demands a contemporary analysis of each congregation, so that God's message through Peter may be proclaimed to it with surgical precision.

The use of the word **refugees** indicates Peter's concern to address himself to the plight of Jews who were—literally—such. This highly connotative term, with all of its emotional overtones,[4] may seem a bit too vivid for a description of the situation in which most of the members of your congregation may find themselves. There are two solutions to this problem:

1. Physical persecution for Christ's sake does exist today in many parts of the world and very readily could be experienced by physically comfortable church members (or their children) to whom the possibility now may seem so remote. Awakening them to that possibility in their lifetime, and preparing them for it *before* the event, is a valid and important use of the book.

2. But the literal use of the word **refugees** in the verse does not preclude the less literal use of the concept (as Peter himself seems to use it by a play upon the idea in 2:11, 12); here the earthly state (in contrast to the heavenly one ushered in at the day of inspection) is considered as transient and unstable as that of a resident alien. The Christian, here and now, whether in physical persecution or not, must face many of the problems of a refugee. He has fled from Satan's Egypt (the land of bondage), but he is still wandering on his journey to the heavenly Jerusalem.

It is possible to preach an entire sermon from verse 1, especially stressing this theme of the suffering, persecuted refugee (and under certain condtions mentioned below, this may seem desirable), but it is neither necessary nor desirable to do so if this is but the first of a series of sermons on the entire book. The purpose of the verse

---

4. Cf. the uses of the word in Moulton & Milligan.

is to say *God understands your plight and cares.* Put a bit more exactly, it is *God has moved His church to know and care about your suffering.* Combining this truth with those expressed in the next verse rounds off a fuller sermon.

who are chosen according to the foreknowledge of God the Father, that by the Spirit's sanctification you may obey and be sprinkled by the blood of Jesus Christ. May help and peace to you be increased! (I Pet. 1:2).

The words in this verse interject themselves into the discussion of the previous verse with force—almost clashing upon them! Suffering refugees, scattered far from their homes by persecution, are here called God's **eternally chosen people!** From eternity past they had been **foreknown by God the Father** as a selected (**chosen**) group especially dear to Him. The fatherly relationship of God to His children in Christ doubtless was interposed by Peter to emphasize His loving concern for them. All that has transpired has taken place as a part of the loving and wise providence of God.

The seeming clash of concepts is deliberate. The world may see the Christian (as, indeed, in moments of discouragement he may see himself) as a defeated, abandoned person about whom nobody cares and for whom there is little hope for the future. By transcending the immediate, and instead referring to the **foreknowledge** of God (God's knowledge of what He intends to do prior to the fact itself) Peter sets aside all doubts and misgivings, and opens new interpretive horizons for those who have become bogged down in the pressures of the moment. God knows about everything; indeed, He has always known. There are no surprises in all of this; it is a part of His purposes. Moreover, as your Father He cares. He has **chosen** you to suffer for the sake of His name and to honor and glorify His Son. You are **refugees** in Pontus, Galatia, Cappadocia, Asia and Bithynia not because of some tragic setback in God's plans; you are there at His bidding. Just as the gospel message was spread in Judea and Samaria by **refugees** fleeing Jerusalem during that first great perse-

7

cution (Acts 8:4), so you too must announce the good news to those where you now reside as **refugees.** There is a witness to be borne and a church to be established where you are.

There will be discouraged, doubting, defeated Christians present in almost any worship service. In preaching from this passage keep that in mind. There will be persons who this week will run into trials that challenge their faith; keep them in mind too. Many counselees come with doubts and complaints; to put matters straight from the outset, lift them from the immediate to the greater purposes of God. Emphasize fully both the encouragement and the responsibility conveyed by verse 2. Let us turn to the rest of the verse to discover how he relates these biblical Siamese twins.

Eternally **chosen** according to God's **foreknown** purposes, these **refugees** (as all Christians) were forgiven and cleansed of their sin **by the blood of Jesus Christ** that was **sprinkled** upon them.[5] This cleansing was effected by the Holy Spirit at a point in time (note the trinitarian emphasis in the two verses—all three Persons of the Trinity share in the new life of the believer), and this resulted in their **sanctification.**[6] To be sanctified means to be set apart by the Spirit as one who is peculiarly His; it is, in short, to become a special person. God **chose** them, redeemed them in Christ, and by His Spirit called them from the world into the fellowship of His redeemed family, the church (literally, the "called out ones").

Peter reminds his readers of these far-reaching facts in order to stress a third point:

1. It is true that God knows and cares about His suffering people;
2. It is also encouraging to know that these sufferings are not the result of some failure on His part, but are (to be sure)

---

5. On the concept of sprinkling as cleansing see Hebrews 9:13, 14, 19, 21, 23.
6. The word **sanctification** here is used not in its theological sense (as the *process* of more and more being set apart from sin unto righteousness). Rather, the word is used in a more definitive sense that views the Christian as already set apart from the world and unto God in Christ. For a similar N.T. usage, cf. Heb. 10:10; 13:12; but see also Heb. 10:14.

a part of His inscrutable purpose for the blessing of those He has chosen from eternity;

3. Moreover, since these two facts are true, it is also true that the suffering that they experience does not relieve them from their responsibility to obey God's commandments. As a matter of fact, if anything, persecution increases responsibilities, calling for additional precautions in new and important situations.

In a manner that has baffled theologians, Peter quite naturally blends the themes of God's eternal purpose (and God's choice of them for salvation) with this insistence upon personal responsibility: they are **chosen** that they may **obey**. The blend is not unique. In passages in which the twin concepts are found in even more vivid juxtaposition, Peter likewise pulls them close together (cf. Acts 2:23; 4:27, 28). With similar ease, we too must teach both sides of this one coin. It has been wrong for theologians to question either one or the other face. The two ideas do not compete. God's eternal plan included not only the desired result (a **sanctified** and **obedient** people) but all the means by which this result would be brought about. In this plan He provided for the creation of responsible human beings—not automatons. *Through*—and not apart from—their responsible actions, these results would occur. He never envisioned the results apart from the means. Human responsibility, *as an element of the divine purpose,* is emphasized by Peter.

Put in concrete terms, Peter teaches that God planned to make them His own people, sent them from their homes into exile for His purposes which he intends them to carry out **obediently.** "You were **chosen** to **obey**," says Peter. A neater balance between sovereign election and human responsibility could not be imagined.

In practical applications, both factors must be emphasized in order to preserve the balance. Failure to do so leads either to a denial of God's control of things (and the despair that follows this conclusion) or a *lassez-faire* attitude expressed in the word *kismet* (with its subsequent antinomianism and hopelessness). "God has led you, His **chosen** ones whom He has set apart for Himself, into suffering for His

9

purposes and your good (Rom. 8:28); therefore, take heart and **obey** Him." That is Peter's fine word.

Obedience in suffering (as we shall see) is a keynote of the book. Combined with trust in the goodness of a Creator-Father Who controls and cares, the major message of I Peter to the suffering saint can be put into the words of the title of the old hymn, *Trust* and *Obey* (cf. I Pet. 4:19).

Since it will be difficult to do so (there is a very welcome realism in this letter that never minimizes suffering, and, on the other hand, that always maximizes the Savior), Peter observes that they will need **help** (grace). So he calls upon God to send **help** and **peace** in even greater measure than they had heretofore experienced (may it be **increased**).

Help and **peace,** together with the addition of one other element that he quickly mentions in verse 3 (**hope**), are precisely what a persecuted sufferer needs! In preaching and in counseling alike, the minister of the word must be certain that he omits none of these essential elements.[7] It does no good to offer **help** to a person who has no **hope.** On the other hand, a person with **hope** will soon lose it if he is not given **help** consisting of concrete directions for achieving what the Bible requires of him when suffering persecution. He also needs strength from the Spirit (Eph. 3:16; I Pet. 5:10) in order to follow directions. **Help** encompasses both direction and power. **Peace** will come to those who know that they are living **obediently** according to God's will, by His **help** and looking expectantly (i.e., in **hope**) for the fulfillment of the glorious promises.[8]

---

7. Inner **peace** before God (even in the midst of outer turmoil) is the proximate goal of counseling (the ultimate goal, of course, is the honor of God), concrete **help** is the means (God often sends help by the ministry of other believers—just as Peter's letter, doubtless, in part, at least, was the answer to their prayers), and **hope** is the motivating factor bringing forth endurance (cf. I Thess. 1:3). For additional information on **hope** and **help** in counseling, see my book, *The Christian Counselor's Manual*.

8. **Hope** in the Bible means "anticipation" or "expectation" of something that God has promised; it never denotes the uncertainty that inheres in the modern English word (often expressed by the phrase, "a hope-so attitude").

10

So then, verses 1 and 2 constitute a preaching unit encompassing key elements essential to proper living in suffering and persecution. While not many who attend services may suffer as refugees, the principles for living through suffering are the same (regardless of the cause for suffering, so long as it is not brought on one's self by his own sin). After all, Peter also mentions other forms of suffering (e.g., from an unsaved marriage partner—chapter 3).

A message from verses 1 and 2 might include the following points (each of which could be expanded into a separate sermon if you were not beginning a series on the entire book, by using examples from the rest of the letter of I Peter under each point):

Introduction: How do you handle suffering, Christian? Your assumptions are basic to how you will face and meet it. What are they? Here are some that should help.

I. GOD KNOWS AND CARES ABOUT YOUR SUFFERING.
II. GOD PLANNED IT FOR YOUR BLESSING.
III. GOD EXPECTS YOU TO OBEY HIM IN IT.
    A. Examples of how people use suffering as an excuse for disobedience.
    B. Suffering increases rather than lessens obligations.
IV. GOD WILL HELP YOU TO OBEY AND GIVE YOU PEACE.

Conclusion: Take heart, suffering Christian, from these truths; go back and face it in a new way.

Be prepared for suffering if you are not suffering now; these truths will help prepare you.

Section Two

Let us praise the God and Father of our Lord Jesus Christ, Who according to His great mercy regenerated us to a living hope through the resurrection of Jesus Christ from the dead, for an incorruptible, unspotted and unfading inheritance that has been kept in the heavens for you who are guarded by God's power through faith for a salvation that is ready to be revealed in the last time (I Pet. 1:3-5).

Even in the midst of persecution and suffering Peter doesn't hesitate to call his readers to praise and thanksgiving. And he does so right away; he doesn't take time to gradually develop his theme. Instead, he plunges right ahead! How can he do so?

First, let it be noted, everything else that he has to say depends upon his readers' attitude toward suffering. Having set forth the truths in verses 1 and 2 as presuppositions for suffering saints, he calls for a basic response to those truths. And there is good reason for praise and thanksgiving, as he has shown and will continue to show in the rest of the chapter.

At the outset he notes the loving care that the heavenly **Father** demonstrated toward His Son Jesus by raising Him from the dead. This fact, in itself, because of its power and wonder, would be enough to elicit praise and thanksgiving, but it is not all. In his concern for the **scattered** suffering sheep, Peter draws out all the pastoral implications of Christ's **resurrection.**

Mercifully, God has given us life (He **regenerated** us) to enable us to see what His **resurrection** means for us. This **regeneration** has resulted in a **living hope** (i.e., a vital expectation—one that has

12

impact upon daily living because of its certainty) that affords **help** even for refugees. This **hope** leads not only to **obedience,** but to **praise.**

Obedience may be of two sorts: grudging or willing. God wants His people to do His will not merely because He says so (such **obedience** may be reluctant and—at times—even grudging); He desires willing, joyful service. Reflection upon the Christian's **hope** is one important way to develop thankful **obedience** given in **praise.**

What is this **hope,** and from what source does it come? In his characteristic way, Peter begins at the nearest point (relating the last effect) and works back toward earlier ones (other earlier effects and prior causes).[9] Accordingly, in verse 3 he reveals hope's *source* while in the next two verses he will consider the hope itself.

The source of the Christian's **hope** is **the reurrection of Jesus Christ from the dead;** if He rose, so shall we. If He, the mediatorial Son of God, entered into this **inheritance,** as fellow-heirs, so shall we (Rom. 8:17).

The Christian's expectation (**hope**) is based upon a solid foundation toward which homeless suffering refugees may look with certainty and joyous anticipation. They are heirs who, when they shall come to their true home (Heb. 11:13-16), will receive an eternal **inheritance** (Heb. 9:15).[10]

The characteristics of this **inheritance** are of great importance to refugees who have lost earthly **inheritances** for Christ's sake. Unlike an earthly inheritance, this eternal life together with its benefits and rewards, is *enduring.* Indeed, it is (1) *indestructible* (**incorruptible, unspotted and unfading**); examples of how earthly inheritances suffer from these three sorts of destruction will make the contrast vivid and memorable) and (2) *secure* (**kept in the heavens for you**). No thief, no robber can steal it away. In Matthew 6: 19, 20, Christ previously made both points about earthly treasures

9. Cf. Margaret Thrall, *Greek Particles in the New Testament* (Grand Rapids: Wm. B. Eerdmans, 1962), pp. 47ff.

10. It is interesting to note the many similar themes running through Hebrews and I Peter, both letters to converted Jews.

(they are destructible and insecure) and contrasted these with heavenly riches.

The Christian's **hope**, then, is an expectation that will be realized. The Christian will not be disappointed or shamed. Not even Satan himself can thwart that hope. It is reserved **in the heavens** (i.e., where God is); the most secure place of all. The use of the phrase **in the heavens** corresponds to our modern use of words: "the White House said . . . , or "Washington thinks. . . ." Reference to the location where he resides is another way of saying that "The President says (thinks). . . ." To speak of the Christian's inheritance as **"kept in the heavens for you,"** then, is to say that it is *kept by God*. Thus Peter assures these Christians that nothing can happen to their inheritance—it is utterly secure because it is in God's keeping.

But what of the heir? Can something happen to him so that at length he will fail to enter into his **inheritance?** It would seem foolish for God to guard what His children might never receive; the indestructibility and security of the **inheritance** itself clearly implies the security of the heir as well. But since there are persons who would focus upon the omission if he did not say so in plain unmistakable terms (as, indeed, there have been even without such an omission), the Spirit also speaks clearly about the heir: he is **guarded by God's power.** What **power** is greater? Paul makes the same point in Romans 8:38, 39. *Nothing* is more powerful than God. Thus the heir also is utterly secure. The **hope** of entering into this **inheritance** is a vital one that is calculated to sustain persecuted, suffering Christians.

The means by which this hope is secured is **faith. God's power** extends even so far as to granting life to believers (**regeneration**). No one believes by his own power (I Cor. 12:3); the natural man (unassisted by God's **regenerating** grace) has no power to do so. **Faith** itself is a gift from God (Eph. 2:8, 9), and God's gifts are without recall (Rom. 11:29); God is not an "Indian giver." The **faith** by which a true believer perseveres until the end *lasts until the end:* it endures till **the last time,** when all the fullness of his **salvation**

14

will be revealed. What he now knows only dimly, and what he possesses only in part (as a down payment), he will receive in its entirety. This **inheritance** is the possession of **salvation** in all its fullness, including entire sanctification and glorification with a purified life in a resurrected and transformed body. It includes all else that has not been made known but will be **revealed in the last time** (i.e., at Christ's coming and during that eternal period that His coming introduces). And this **inheritance** (or **salvation** in its fullness) is **ready** now. The believer will not have to wait for it. Neither will he receive it in stages. As one package—as a grand and glorious whole (that will take all eternity to fathom in its fullness)—he will receive it. It is **ready** and waiting for him.

In preaching or in counseling about the **hope** held forth in these verses, it is clear that the emphasis should fall upon indestructibility and security of both the **inheritance** and the heir. The great truth is that the Christian's **hope** will not fail. In the context of suffering it is important to stress the **hope** (with all that it means: negatively, the cessation of sin and its consequences—which you may wish to spell out—and positively, the reception of a sinless life of perfection with all of its blessings—this too could be spelled out concretely) and its certainty. A persecuted person, cast adrift as a **refugee** in a foreign land, quickly discovers the uncertainty and insecurity of temporal hopes. He may become cynical and fear to place his **hope** in anything (or anyone)—he has had his hopes up before only to have them come crashing down around his feet time and again. That hurts—and he doesn't want to be hurt again. While wanting to **hope,** he may hesitate to **hope.** Against all possible misunderstandings, and flung into the face of any such cynicism, to alleviate any and all doubts, Peter has piled word upon word to establish a solid foundation that points to the utter reliability of the believer's basic **hope.** There can be no reasonable doubt about what he says or about its certainty; both the clarity of his words and the assurances given preclude either. The **hope** can be rejected only by rejecting the gospel itself (something that this passage plainly says a believer will never do; cf. also Heb. 6:9).

15

One way to outline the material we have discussed follows:

Introduction: Christian, to help you endure the persecution and suffering in faith to the end—

  I. GOD HAS GIVEN YOU A GREAT HOPE
    A. that is living,
    B. that is based on Christ's resurrection,
    C. and that consists of the inheritance of the fullness of salvation.
  II. GOD GIVES AN INHERITANCE THAT IS CERTAIN
    A. because it is indestructible,
    B. and because it is guarded by God.
  III. GOD PROMISES ALSO TO PRESERVE YOU
    A. through perseverance in faith,
    B. until the last time,
    C. by His own almighty power.

Conclusion: Praise Him for what He has ready and waiting for you in the heavens, and let that hope influence your life today in times of trial and suffering.

Section Three

You should be glad about this even if now you may have to be sad because of many kinds of trials so that the testing of your faith, much more valuable than perishable gold (yet it is tested by fire), may be found to praise and glorify and honor Jesus Christ at His revelation. You haven't seen Him, but you love Him, you don't now look on Him but you believe on Him, and you rejoice with inexpressible and glorious delight, receiving that which is the purpose of your faith —the salvation of your souls (I Pet. 1:6-9).

The theme of these remarkable verses is "Be **glad** when you are **sad!**" Peter does not want you to be **glad** *that* you are **sad;** there is no such teaching in the Scriptures; the miseries of sin are always acknowledged to be just that—misery. Sin's consequences are quite fully and realistically recognized; they are never minimized. What then does Peter mean when he says **you should be glad about this even if now you may have to be sad?** He is saying that the Christian's **hope** is so glorious that when he contrasts it with those sufferings that **sadden** him, he has reason for gladness in spite of the severity of the **trials** that he must endure. In this respect, Paul's words about hope and suffering in Romans 8:18-25 exactly parallel Peter's. A sermon from this passage will gain in depth from reference to Romans 8, especially to verse 18.

I say that Peter's words in verse 6 are realistic. For one thing, he doesn't teach that the **gladness** totally supersedes the **sadness,** as though the former eliminated the latter; rather, he says **gladness** can coexist side by side with **sadness, be glad . . . even if you now may have to be sad.** There are times when suffering brings sadness, and it is not wrong to express that sadness. Every emotion God has given us is good and may be properly expressed. (It will be expressed properly when it is expressed in accordance with biblical guidelines.)

Peter paints no picture of grinning sufferers. That concept (together with its flippant "praise the Lord anyway" attitude) is foreign to the passage. What he does teach is that even in the midst of **many kinds of trials** (it doesn't matter which kind—*all* are included) that at times may bring exquisite **sadness,** the believer need never despair. Instead, he can take heart and be **glad** because he knows that God will fulfill His promises. That is what the Christian hope can do.

In drawing out the congregation to think about the vitality of their hope, you may want to open the message with a series of pointed questions: "How do you take suffering? Do you cry and go all to pieces? Do you grimly bear it? Do you begin to question God (Why did this have to happen to me?)? What, if anything, sustains you in times of sorrow?," etc. Then, you might say, "Did you know that God says you can be **glad** when you are **sad?** You didn't? Well, as a matter of fact, He not only says that this is a possibility— He *requires* it: 'You *should* be **glad** . . . etc.' "

The verse also suggests that Christians suffer **many kinds of trials,** yet can be **glad** in them all. He allows no one to say, "Yes, I think it may be possible to be **glad** in *other* trials, but not in mine." This is important, since some say, "Well, I can bear up under trials at work, I can handle social persecution well enough, but I come unglued when my children turn on me. Are you sure that a full realization of what my **hope** in Christ involves at such times will not only see me through the trial, but even make me **glad** in the midst of sorrow?" Yes. "Then, just what is this full **salvation** that is to be revealed?" It is, of course, many things. But one thing that it is important to know about it in time of trial is that it means both the cessation of all that is now making you **sad** (cf. Rev. 21:4) and the final explanation of why God, in His wise providence, brought this particular **trial** into your life.

18

Not every reason for each **trial** that a Christian suffers can be known prior to that Day, but one reason—because of its obvious effects—can be: **trial** purifies believers by **testing** their **faith.** The impurities in one's **faith** are burned out just as the impurities in **gold** (the dross) are removed by **fire.** The **fires** of persecution especially effect this result in those who endure. As possessions and even loved ones may be taken away, and as physical and social persecution may become added causes of **sadness,** the believer is cast more fully upon God Himself. **Faith** is purified through dependence (a most important element of **faith**) and shines more brightly because of the **fire.** Although **gold** is **valuable, faith** is **much more valuable than perishable gold.** So, then, if **gold** (even though it is not as **valuable** as the Christian's **faith**) must be **tested by fire** to purify it in order to bring out its full value, so too must **faith** in order to bring out its even greater values. When it is refined by the process, the believer's faith all the more will bring **praise, glory and honor to Jesus Christ at His revelation.**

Mention of Jesus' **revelation** (that event in which He will be publicly revealed as the Great God and Savior; Tit. 2:13) reminds Peter that his readers have never **seen Him.** At the **revelation** they will do so for the first time. He comments on the fact, noting that (nevertheless) they **love Him** and **believe on Him,** and that this—not only on that future occasion but even now—should lead to **joy** and **delight** that are **inexpressible** and **glorious** when they reflect on the fact that their **faith** has led to **the salvation of their souls.** The body too will be redeemed in the resurrection, but now—even in the midst of bodily affliction—they know that Christ's promises are sure because they have already received, by **faith, the salvation of their souls.**

The **soul** in the Scriptures is the spirit thought of *in relationship to* (or in union with) the body. The spirit is the **soul** thought of *out of relationship to* (or as disunited from) the body. It is the disembodied **soul.** The immaterial side of a human being is more frequently identified in the Bible as the heart (and as the mind). Each one of these words designates a special way of thinking about the same entity.

19

Mind refers to thought, decision, stance and attitude; *heart* means the inner life that one lives in his own presence before God. Sometimes **soul** simply refers to the animating factor, and is best translated "life." Here (as in Matt. 10:28; III John 2) it cannot mean merely life. **Salvation** of the **soul** refers to the inner renewal effected by the Holy Spirit in **regeneration.** The **soul** was saved (rescued, salvaged) from the perilous condition mentioned in Matthew 10:28. It was corrupted by sin and held guilty and in imminent danger of eternal death. But Christ has given life and faith to the **soul,** freed it from its bondage to Satan and released it to serve God in joy and freedom.

Why does Peter use the somewhat unusual phrase **the salvation of your souls?** Probably because many of these persons to whom he writes were in danger of losing their lives, their bodies would be maimed and disfigured, and (in general) the outer man would be in for difficult times. But the **soul,** unlike the body, in part had already been redeemed (the redemption of the body is yet future—Rom. 8:23-25), so it could transcend suffering and experience **joy** and **delight** in the midst of it.

Introduction: So then, Christian, when you meet suffering

   I. REALISTICALLY: YOU MUST ENTER INTO THE TRUE SADNESS OF IT,
  II. HOPEFULLY: YOU MUST SEE GOD'S GREAT FUTURE IN CONTRAST TO IT, and
 III. JOYFULLY: YOU MUST TRANSCEND IT BY FAITH.

Conclusion: The new life within (a **soul,** or heart, being renewed daily by the Holy Spirit) means that it is possible to be **glad** when you are **sad** because by it you look past suffering in faith to the **glorious** and **inexpressible inheritance** of which your **soul's salvation** is the firstfruits.

Section Four

It was concerning this salvation that the prophets who prophesied about the grace that would be yours searched and sought, trying to find out to what or what period the Spirit of Christ in them pointed when he testified beforehand about the sufferings of Christ and the glories that would follow them. To them it was revealed that they were serving not themselves but you in these things that now have been declared to you through those who, by the Holy Spirit sent from heaven, announced the good news to you, things that the angels desire to look into (I Pet. 1:10-12).

As Peter writes, one thought suggests another. He has mentioned the **salvation** of their **souls**. Now, he elaborates on that **salvation**, showing how very great it is—**prophets** of old and even **angels** wanted to know about it.

They are neither forgotten nor forsaken. These events—including the sufferings they were experiencing—had been long foretold. They are part of a glorious plan of grace that all the ages have been moving toward and about which heaven and earth are deeply concerned. Forgotten? Of course not; these are the days of destiny. These are the days of fulfillment. Rejoice with the **angels** and **prophets**—God's grace is yours in Christ!

First, Peter flatly asserts the fact of prophecy. The **prophets** had written about the **grace** (unmerited favor—here: the saving mercy of God to sinful men who deserved hell) that was planned for his readers (and those who follow). What they wrote, they did not fully understand, nor did they know about whom they were writing. So they **searched** and **sought** to **try to find out** to **what** events and to

21

what **period** of time their revelations referred. (This search clearly indicates that they wrote by a power beyond themselves; they were able to write things they themselves couldn't understand apart from revelation.) They were told (by **revelation**) that their prophetic ministry was for others who would live in future generations, beginning (indeed) with those alive at the time Peter wrote.

It is instructive to notice that the O.T. writers *knew* that the **Spirit of Christ** (an unusual phrase that means the Holy Spirit **testified** about **Christ**) was in them guiding their writing. Their words were the **testimony** (or witness) of the Spirit Himself, not merely their own interpretation of events to come. Peter's words clearly point to a revelatory event of which the **prophets** themselves were cognizant. The often occurring words, "The burden of the Lord came to me saying, . . ." similarly point to such a knowledge. Contrary to modern unbelief—according to which every other explanation of prophecy has been given—the N.T. writers with naturalness and simplicity merely assume the inspiration of the Scriptures. Peter doesn't argue for inspiration, he assumes it and encourages his readers on the basis of the fact. That they too held such a view is clear; otherwise, his mere allusion to inspiration would not do; they would have required an elaborate explanation of the teaching.

The **Spirit** not only was **in them testifying beforehand** (i.e., giving them a prophetic revelation of the future), but He is said to have repeated His revelatory work in the apostles **who . . . announced the good news** to them. Possibly, Peter here is thinking of the apostolic writings (that paralleled the prophetic Scriptures) as well as the inspired apostolic words; cf. Mark 13:11: "Rather, say whatever is given to you in that hour (it won't be you speaking, but the Holy Spirit)." Surely the one was the basis for the other.

The message that the **prophets** proclaimed **beforehand** consisted of a prediction of **Christ's** sacrificial death (Peter calls it **sufferings** since he wants to speak about Christ's way of facing **suffering** later on in the letter as an example and encouragement for his readers), and of His resurrection, ascension and coronation (Peter calls these **the glories that would follow them** [the **sufferings**] in order to contrast the glory that was Christ's—and will be theirs someday—with the present sufferings they were undergoing). His point is that **sufferings** for God lead to **glory** from God. Glory is an important word for Peter and for the sufferers to whom he was writing. Again Romans 8:18 is apropos; see also Hebrews 2:10. This is the same good news that Paul likewise found in the O.T. and which he likewise formulated into a twofold proclamation:

1. that Christ died for our sins *in agreement with the Scriptures;*
2. that He was buried, and that He was raised on the third day *in agreement with the Scriptures* (I Cor. 15:3, 4).

Throughout the book of Acts the news of Christ's death and resurrection is the standard evangelistic proclamation: cf. 2:23, 24; 3: 13-15; 4:10; 5:29-32; 10:39-41; 13:28-33; 26:23.

Peter says that the Holy Spirit was active in giving **revelation** both in the O.T. period and after He had been **sent from heaven** on the Day of Pentecost. The **Spirit of Christ** is the **Spirit** Who constantly testifies, not about Himself, but about **Christ** (John 16:13, 14).

The great point of the passage again is to offer encouragement for suffering saints. Wonderful things have been promised by God in the coming fullness of salvation. Knowledge of this salvation comes not from human sources—great teachers, scientists, philosophers—but directly from God Himself. Peter, as we have seen, is not teaching the doctrine of the inspiration of the Scriptures (he assumes it everywhere—that is all the more powerful an assertion of it), but is urging his readers to consider the encouragement that the inspired prophecies should bring.

He says,

Introduction: You are suffering? Do you think God has forgotten or forsaken you? Well, consider this:

I. GOD PROPHESIED ABOUT THESE DAYS LONG AGO
   A. In inspired writings
   B. By the Spirit Who testifies about Christ.

II. GOD TOLD THE PROPHETS THAT THEY WERE SERVING YOU.
    A. They sought to discover what they were predicting.
    B. They sought to discover the period they were predicting.
    C. And God told them they were predicting His grace to you.
III. GOD PREDICTED SUFFERING FOR HIM LEADS TO GLORIES
    A. In Christ's death and resurrection.
    B. In your lives too.

Conclusion: Rejoice! What you are experiencing is the subject of angelic interest.

Section Five

Therefore, buckling the belts of your minds for action, keeping level-headed, set your hope entirely on the grace that will be brought to you at the revelation of Jesus Christ (I Pet. 1:13).

The encouragement that comes in suffering is not mystical; it doesn't just suddenly appear from nowhere. The Christian himself is responsible for it. If he doesn't experience the joy, gladness, hope, etc., mentioned in the previous verses, that is his *own* fault. He cannot complain against God, the church, or anyone else; this verse makes it perfectly plain that *he* is responsible for developing the hope that will sustain him in trial. Counselees (the typical hopeless counselee blames everyone but himself) as well as others need to learn this fact. This, then, is an all-important message to communicate. Very few Christians realize the fact.

Encouragement in trial is not merely a matter of trusting in God's promises in some purely intellectual manner. Surely that is important—indeed, it is a theme that Peter never really leaves behind—but there is another side to the page; the suffering believer must do good (this theme also runs throughout the letter). And that doing of good (not to be saved, but growing out of salvation for God's glory) begins with the matter of **hope**. Right here, at the outset, the believer's trust in God's promises is pictured as a matter of obedience: **set your hope on the grace. . . .** That is a command, involving a duty. Consistent with the major thrust of the entire epistle, Peter already strikes the note: *Trust and Obey!* There is no other way to be happy in trial, but to trust and obey. This is God's way. God holds the individual believer responsible for his

25

behavior in times of trial and trouble and says that these two elements constitute that responsibility. They also provide God's path to power and witness. So, then, in verse 13, Peter turns the page and begins to stress *action*. And this opens with a **therefore**, which links what he is about to say to all that he has written thus far. This **therefore** refers the reader back to the sure expectancy of the coming glories of the believer's inheritance. He says,

Therefore,

> **Set your hope entirely on the grace that will be brought to you at the revelation of Jesus Christ;**

and he explains how this may (must) be done:

> **buckling the belts of your minds for action, keeping level-headed** [or sober].

These are exciting words, and the counselor or preacher who uses them must convey all the power and force of that excitement to his hearer. There is nothing slow moving or pedestrian here; to slacken the pace or reduce the punch is to distort the meaning and lessen the impact. Throw this fast-ball with all your might right across the center of the plate, knee-high! This pitch has plenty of stuff on it; give it all you've got!

The Greeks, and other orientals who lived among them, wore long robes that made strenuous effort requiring **action** difficult. So, when preparing for **action**—work, battle, etc.—they would gather up their skirts and tuck them into their belts to get them out of the way (cf. I Kings 18:46). That is what Peter had in mind when he wrote these words (which are equivalent to our "roll up your sleeves," or **buckle your belts**). The idea behind the figure is to *prepare for action.*

But Peter boldly extends the figure to *mental* action: **buckle up the belts of your *minds* for action.** The picture is highly suggestive: there is mental work to do; mental battles to be fought. Action must be taken in your **mind.** Here the word for **mind** is *dianoia* (a word that signifies thinking *through* questions; the term has to do with the use of the intellect in reaching an understanding of problems).

26

Peter is calling on his (your) hearers to be more than passive listeners to the Word; they must actively think through the meaning of what they hear and determine how it applies to their own situaion. Action—hard mental work and struggle—are essential for maintaining and fostering **hope** in days of difficulty and times of trouble. **Trials** cannot be overcome successfully by a passive attitude; they are fought through in the **mind** (cf. also my book, *How to Overcome Evil*, in which this theme is amplified considerably).

So, Peter calls on his readers to prepare their **minds** for mental **action** (that too is essentially what you should do in the use of this verse in counseling or in preaching). They must tackle serious problems for Jesus Christ. Every trial calls for careful biblical analysis, remembering (or discovering) scriptural truths and principles, and determining the concrete application of these to actual life situations. Thus the Christian refugee will have well-thought-through answers to give anyone who asks a reason for the **hope** that is in him (cf. I Pet. 3:15).

Living as a Christian at all times—but especially during times of extreme pressure—requires the use of the mind (the intellectual processes). Contrary to emphases in the Eastern religions, the **mind** of the Christian is not by-passed, but is central in all that he does. He is a person of the Book. In that Book is a revelation from God that he must become entirely familiar with and that he must understand and apply to daily affairs. That demands mental work—and struggle! The Christian cannot expect to please God if he is not willing to work hard at thinking. The great emphasis upon experience and emotion that is overwhelming Western society (and many evangelical churches too!) is sheer poison because it leads to interpretation of God's truth through experience rather than interpretation of experience through God's truth. The Bible must interpret experience; it may not be interpreted by it. Of course, experience may issue the call for biblical interpretation—it does *all the time*—but the interpreter must develop a very sensitive exegetical conscience by which he is able to come to the well with an empty bucket to draw the pure water of life. Much thought, mental struggle, etc., lie behind such willingness. But that is what Peter (the Holy Spirit, writing through him) demands. The believer who refuses to think, who takes the course of least resistance (drifting with the crowd or circumstances) or follows his feelings, sins against God. Christianity places no premium on ignorance; it is (as its history exhibits) not anti-intellectual.

Second, Peter tells how the believer must approach his intellectual work and engage in mental struggle—**level-headedly.** The word also can mean "soberly," but Peter is not thinking of literal drunkenness. If you wish to push the figure in the word, the way to make the point is to say that he is urging his hearers to avoid becoming intoxicated with any and all concerns that would hinder calm, cool and steady deliberation in sorrow or crisis. The level-headed Christian doesn't let feelings overcome thought. His actions and feelings are kept under control. His feelings are used as his servant rather than becoming the master of his behavior. Nothing clouds or overwhelms his mind. Thus, at all times, he is able to act in accordance with his best judgments of what he knows from the Bible.

Lastly, Peter urges the need to *set* **hope on future grace. Hope**— it is clear from this—doesn't come automatically. One must nurture and develop **hope** by using his **mind** in a **level-headed** manner to learn, understand, contemplate and apply the facts of Scripture (especially those already set forth in this chapter; remember the **therefore**). The verb **set hope on** is an aorist imperative that carries the thrust of *once for all* doing so. The action is pictured as occurring all at one point in time; not strung out over time as a process. The reader is, therefore, called upon to decide for this way of life and to embark upon it. This is a matter of forsaking all else, turning one's back on all other approaches to the problem of handling persecution and suffering, and depending wholly upon this biblical mode of action.

The expectation upon which the Christian must **entirely set hope** is the **grace** (already referred to as the **salvation** and **inheritance**) that **Jesus Christ** will **bring** at His second coming when He is **revealed** before the entire universe as the great God and Savior (Tit. 2:3). This is the time of His glory.

To hope is not merely a privilege; it is also a duty (Peter commands it). At first, this may seem strange to your hearers who, in this feeling-oriented age, have been taught that hope and love (some even think of faith this way) are basically feelings; these things just "happen." They are not connected in any way to responsible action or intellectual processes. But you must make it clear to them that such thinking isn't biblical. Peter plainly views hope as a duty that can be fulfilled by obedient believers when they follow the directions of the Scriptures. When a counselee lacks hope, one may sympathize with his pitiable state since to be without hope, indeed, is a sad condition. But he may not fail to confront him with the fact that this lack of hope is his own doing. It is the result of sin, sinful disobedience to God's command. The counselor's (or preacher's) stance must be sympathetic disagreement (cf. the article on this in my book, *What About Nouthetic Counseling?*) He may sympathize with his miserable state, but disagree with his (usually) irresponsible attitude about it (often expressed in bitterness and blame shifting). Hope, the counselor will observe, comes when one reads, understands and depends upon God's promises; it develops in the hearts of believers who prepare their minds for action. It belongs to those who willingly fight the intellectual battles that will capture their minds for Christ. Any believer without hope lacks it because of wilful ignorance, disobedience or unbelief. God hasn't failed to make adequate promises in Scripture from which he could take heart! As a matter of fact, Peter's command to set hope on God's grace *itself* should bring hope:

(1) God never commands His children to do anything that He does not provide the directions to do (in Scripture) and the power to follow them by His Spirit;

(2) If hope is commanded, one need not sit and wait for it; rather, by obedience he can have it. It is available!

In this verse, Peter also urges single-mindedness when he writes set your hope *entirely* on the grace. . . . There can be no double-minded approach to the matter. The concentration of focus envisioned in the word entirely (the Greek also may be translated "perfectly," "fully," or "completely") refers to a sweeping aside of all other hopes, especially those temporal expectations which in the end can lead only to discouragement or despair since they have no substance to them. There must be no vacillation;[11] persecution and trial admit of few second chances. There is one—and only one—source for the Christian's **hope**: the promises and prophecies of the future found in the very same inspired Book that sustained the prophets in trial as they sought and searched its pages.

In counseling, as I have shown in a number of my books,[12] lack of hope comes from trusting the Bible partially. When one puts partial faith in the Scriptures and partial faith in the schemes of men, he denudes the Bible promises by hinging them to human hopes and promises that are destined to fail. So important is this matter of **setting one's hope** *entirely* on God's promises that Peter has placed the word **entirely** in an emphatic position. In reading and teaching this verse, the word should be strongly emphasized.

It is instructive for a pastor-teacher to know that the Bible *stresses* the important part that a working knowledge of God's provisions for eternity plays in the believer's present life. Lack of preaching (or other instruction) about the future blessings prepared for the Christian will lead to weakness and inability to meet trials and crises. Peter is not alone in making the connection; John plainly does so too in I John 3:1-3 (esp. vs. 3). And that is one reason why great promises (note that there are such in every one of the seven letters to the seven churches) of God's future blessing are held out in the book of Revelation to Christians who would have to "overcome" in times of terrifying persecution.[13] If, in considering your own teaching/preaching ministry, pastor, you discover a lack of emphasis upon

---

11. The sort of instability to which James refers in his letter (1:8) must be avoided. An important historical instance of such vacillation (or double-mindedness) is recorded in I Kings 18 (see especially vs. 21). The people had little or no hope in God's promises because they limped between two opinions. Thorough investigation of the facts followed by a wholehearted commitment to Jehovah was the answer, Elijah said.

12. See especially appropriate sections in *Lectures on Counseling* and *The Christian Counselor's Manual*.

13. For more on this, see my book, *The Time Is at Hand*.

the great hopes God has given His people, it is time to remedy this situation. If you detect a failure on the part of members of your congregation to handle trials well God's way, it may be that (1) there has been too little of such instruction in the past, (2) the connection between expectancies of blessing and present endurance of affliction has not been made clear enough, (3) there has been no call for a deliberate, decisive **setting of hope** upon God's **grace,** or (4) there is a rebellious and disobedient spirit among those who have heard but won't act. It would not be wise to conclude that suggestion four is the reason until suggestions one through three first have been explored to the full.

Peter wants to make unmistakably clear, lest anyone forget it, the fact that not only all that we now have, but also all that we shall receive at the **revelation** of **Christ** is unmerited; that is why he calls it **grace. Grace** is God's merciful, loving, undeserved gift. And to emphasize the on-going nature of this **grace** (as well as its enormity) he says it **will be brought to you.** When God does something for His children, He doesn't do it half way. In mercy, He *brings* the inheritance to them in His Son **Jesus Christ,** Who—amazing though it may seem— will allow us to share His glory with Him on His day at the **revelation** ("unveiling") of His glory! That is grace upon grace!

I have isolated this one verse as a preaching portion because it is pivotal. It forms a summary of and conclusion to all that has gone before, calling for action. It is a tightly constructed sentence, packed full of weighty content. And it provides a hinge (again, note the **therefore**) for hooking the great promises of the first twelves verses of the letter to the more practical applications and exhortations that follow. Because it calls for mental action (**set your hope on . . .** by **buckling . . . your minds** and **keeping level-headed**), it provides a good opportunity to draw the net on what you have been teaching in the previous sermons as well as what you may say additionally in this one. Indeed, a good series of messages on Christian hope could be preached from I Peter 1:1-13 without going on to preach from the rest of the letter.

The major portion of this verse (don't forget) is to summon believers (who haven't done so) to **set their hopes on** the future **grace** of God. They, together with others whose **hopes** have been **set** on that **grace,** must do so in two ways:

(1) by thinking more deeply about God's promises (**buckle the belts of your minds for action**) in order to understand their meaning and application to present distresses more fully than ever before—here is something *all* Christians can engage in. And it ought to be done very concretely ("What, really, does the promise of a new body mean to me, an arthritis sufferer?" or, "How does the full revelation of Christ's glory relate to the rejection of my witness about Him by my fellow college students?"),

(2) and by **keeping level-headed** (not allowing emotion, cares or other concerns to sweep aside the truths that believers need to sustain them in trial. A good parallel passage is Matthew 13:18-23, the parable of the sower. Christ says that **the right sort of ground is the person who** *hears* **the message and** *understands* **it.** Clearly, in contrast, verses 19-22 refer to those who **hear,** but **don't understand,** to those who **hear** but allow **affliction or persecution** to drive the message away, and to those who **hear** but by **worry** and by the love of **money**—and these two also are linked in Matthew 6—choke the **seed** so that it cannot grow. The **level-headed** Christian will be aware of these problems and by God's direction and strength prayerfully will avoid them. He will be steady in trial and in temptation, whether the latter comes from without or from within).

Here is one way of approaching the passage (and, as in all these outlines, there is nothing more than a sketch; a full outline would include much more):

Introduction: Hope (we have seen) is important for suffering Christians; if you don't have hope, that's your fault; you can blame no one but yourself, so . . .

  I. SET YOUR HOPE ON GOD'S GRACE.
    A. Does it surprise you that God commands hope?
    B. It wouldn't if you hadn't been influenced by the modern, feeling-oriented view of hope.
    C. Hope isn't a feeling that happens; but a duty that can be fulfilled.
    D. And it is to be *set* on God's grace (explain).

How?
  II. BUCKLE THE BELT OF YOUR MIND FOR ACTION.
    A. You must get ready to do some serious thinking
    B. About this grace,
    C. What it should mean to you
    D. And precisely how it may be applied to change your attitudes and behavior.

And . . .
  III. KEEP LEVEL-HEADED.
    A. So that you won't be turned aside from that hope by other concerns or experience-based action,
    B. By setting your hope *entirely* on God's grace
    C. And letting that hope affect all your attitudes and actions.

Conclusion: Once for all—right now—assume the responsibility for your hope and set it where it should be—on God's coming grace.

Section Six

As children who are under obedience, don't shape your lives by the desires that you used to follow in your ignorance. Instead, as the One Who called you is holy, you yourselves must become holy in all your behavior. I say this because it is written: "You must be holy because I am holy" (I Pet. 1:14-16).

Peter has spoken profoundly about the need for deliberate mental **action** in the midst of trial and suffering, and has stressed the need for **level-headedness** (cool, non-emotional decision making). Now, even more explicitly he emphasizes the importance of **obedience** and the need to reject the old ways of decision making and the development of response patterns that **shape** one's **life** by following feelings (**desires**). Such behavior, he notes, comes from **ignorance** of the true meaning and proper way to use the Scriptures. It does not come from thoughtful, **obedient** action based upon God's commandments found in His Word (cf. comments on vs. 13).

Peter wants his readers (and yours) to recognize the vital fact that they are **children under obedience**. God's children do not have the right to make their own decisions about how they will conduct their **lives.** Left to themselves, sinful children (as we have seen all too frequently) will follow their **desires.** That is because sinners are, by virtue of their sinful natures, self-centered. But God wants His redeemed children to be other-centered. He wants them to love Him and their neighbors (the sum and substance of His commandments). God, therefore, has not left His children to themselves; they are **under obedience** (i.e., obligated to obey Him as their heavenly Father); they are not of age. This theme will be picked up again in verse 17. As a good Father, God has set up rules and drawn the guidelines for the behavior of His **children.** All of these are given by direct revelation in the Bible. Pastor, how are your people **shaping their lives?** Just look at the **shape** that many of them are in and you will know—there can be no doubt about it! They allow fads, fashions (the word **shape** in the original implies temporariness, changeableness) and feelings to do so. Whatever *others* think they do, since they are motivated by **desire** (they lust after the things others possess and even do what they really don't want to do because of social pressures; it doesn't feel good to be criticized or ostracized). That is how unbelievers live (cf. Eph. 4:17f.); they can't do otherwise. But believers also can relapse into similar styles of life if they do not carefully seek to understand and **obediently** endeavor to follow the Scriptures. In the final analysis, there are but two (and *only* two) ways of shaping one's life:

    (1) by **obedience** to God's Word, or

    (2) by following one's own **desires.**

Since all of society is oriented toward the second approach and since the flesh (old pagan ways of life brought into the new life of a believer) also tends in that direction, it is easy to fall into such temptations. Only regular, conscious, prayerful obedience to the Bible can enable one to make headway against these powerful forces.

Because the believer's **mind** is being **renewed** (Eph. 4:23; Rom. 12:1, 2) in order to enable him to overcome the **desires** of the flesh by **putting off** the **old person** (Eph. 4:22) and **putting on** the **new person** (Eph. 4:24), he no longer needs to live according to feelings (as vs. 18 indicates, he has been **set free** from bondage to such **behavior patterns**).

The unbeliever acts in **ignorance;** he is driven about by every whim of feeling (cf. Eph. 4:18). But the believer is no longer bound by **ignorance;** his **mind** is being **renewed** in **true righteousness and holiness** (Eph. 4:24) according to *knowledge* (Col. 3:10). This means he can begin to reflect his heavenly Father's image once more in his life. This means that it is now possible for him to **walk by the Spirit** so that he doesn't **accomplish the desires of the flesh**[14] (Gal. 5:16). Thus it is possible to **put on the Lord Jesus Christ** (i.e., to think, act and speak like Him) instead of making **plans to satisfy the desires of the flesh** (Rom. 13:14).

What question could be more important to a Christian than how he **shapes** his life? Yet how many have ever considered it? How many could tell you if you asked? By the conclusion of your sermon (or counseling session) all that should have changed; every Christian who heard not only should know how he has been doing so, but how to do so in the future. Moreover, he should be so convicted and concerned (if not committed) about this matter that throughout the weeks to come—until the way of obedience becomes habitual—he should regularly stop and ask himself, "How am I making this **life-shaping** decision?[15] According to God's commandments or my own feelings and wishes (desires)?" Hardly any other matter could be more basic; strongly press the question.

But notice, these words were written to *suffering* saints. In suffering, emotional factors like sorrow, pain and loss tend to play a large part in living. So others are likely to excuse deviant **desire**-oriented behavior on the basis of extenuating circumstances. But God doesn't! Instead, He calls for strict obedience. Indeed, if there ever were a time for **obedient** living it is during persecution. Like a soldier, trained to obey in battle, he must be prepared for obedient living when his feelings and wishes most strongly push for the opposite. Following feelings leads directly to compromises with sin, including a denial of the Lord (Peter knew all too well from previous experience that denial results from **shaping** life by desire and feeling). Unless he has become accustomed to denying **desires** and obeying God in other situations, the believer will fail during times of extreme pressures.

How can a Christian become conscious of the need to live a life

---

14. For a detailed study of Paul's use of *flesh,* see my *Lectures on Counseling,* pp. 231ff.

15. Life-shaping decisions are not all life-shaking ones. Life is shaped largely by many small decisions in everyday affairs strung together into patterns.

of **obedience?** By remembering his true status. He is not yet of age; he is still a minor—a **child** who is **under obedience** (i.e., he is subject to his Father Whom he must honor by obeying; cf. Eph. 6:1).

And, in this case, his **Father** is the **holy** heavenly **Father,** into Whose likeness and image he is being renewed (Eph. 4:24; Col. 3:10). In **all his behavior** he is to be like His **Father** Who is **holy.** He was called by Him to **holiness,** to become like Him. And this accords with biblical teaching: Leviticus 11:44, 45; 19:2; 20:7. The standard for Christian Living is God Himself: like Father, like son.

But what is **holiness?** That question has provided unnecessary problems for Christians over the years. Most of these problems have resulted from attempts to make the Bible conform to erroneous ecclesiastical practices and from theological speculation. The concept of **holiness** in the Bible is not complex; it is quite simple.

Fundamentally, both the Hebrew and Greek words have a similar root meaning: separateness. In the Scriptures words from this root have been translated to *hallow,* to *sanctify, holy* and *saint.* In every case—regardless of these differing translations—the concept of separateness prevails. A saint is one that God has separated from others to set him apart for Himself. Thus His people are said to be a **holy** people (cf. 2:9) who are His, and His alone. Even the pots and pans in the temple were called **holy** (they were set apart for temple use alone; an Israelite couldn't borrow them to fry his bacon and eggs in—especially the bacon!). This last usage plainly shows that the idea of moral behavior (so frequently equated with holiness today) was secondary. When God's people are exhorted to be **holy** as God is **holy,** then it means that as He is unique (separate or different from all others; there is no god like Him; cf. Ex. 15:11—the first use of the word **holy** with reference to God—where such a comparison is made) so too must they be in all their living. The Christian must be *different.* Separateness or difference from others who do not bear a family relationship to God, is the fundamental idea. God's children, like Him, must be different.

Now, as the context shows, the **holiness** (difference) *secondarily* has to do with morality (cf. vss. 14, 17, 22, etc.). This is stated

37

clearly in verse 15: **you must become holy** (separate, different) **in all your behavior.** This idea runs through the rest of the letter, and surfaces from time to time through the rest of the letter (note esp. 4:1-4). Because what God does is different from all the false gods, His children's behavior must differ from the behavior of their children. God wants a **holy** (different) family.

The difference that God requires of His children takes place when they **obediently shape their lives** according to God's commandments rather than their own desires. In the passage the stress on **obedience** implies following God's commandments; but the passage also makes God's **holiness** the ground for **holy** living: **be holy because I am holy.** The two go together. It is God's holiness that is foundational to His commandments. And since that is true, those who follow His commandments become **holy** like Him.

Peter is careful to insist on uniqueness **in all your behavior.** That leaves nothing out of the picture. Across the board, the Christian life must be different. That includes the entire spectrum of life—social, educational, business, family, physical life, etc. The difference is not restricted to the ethical or religious spheres alone. Consequently, in everything he does, the Christian should act differently from those in the world around him. It is not that he tries to be different merely for the sake of novelty. Rather, the more obediently he applies biblical truth to every aspect of living, the more nearly unique his life style will be *without trying.* He is to be wholly holy.

It is interesting to notice how Peter uses the O.T. in verse 16. For him, it is authoritative and (therefore) final. The point is clinched by the mere quotation of an appropriate text. This "proof-texting" (as it is often derisively labeled) is not infrequent in the N.T. When obviously appropriate material that should be clearly convincing to any sensitive Christian is cited in such a manner, there is no reason whatever why such a use of the Scriptures cannot be made. Sometimes the pseudo-sophistication of the critics and scholars who denounce the use of *all* proof texts amounts to nothing more or less than sheer arrogance.

What has Peter said in these three verses? He has called for unique (different, holy) behavior from God's children, behavior that reflects favorably upon their heavenly Father, Who also acts differently. Such behavior can be developed by uniquely shaping their lives by obedience rather than by following feelings and desires. Here is one way it might be presented:

Introduction: Aren't you tired of the sameness around you? God has called you to a life of uniqueness.
Christian . . .

    I. YOU HAVE A GOD WHO IS DIFFERENT.
       A. He is holy (explain).
       B. He is unlike all the false gods.
       C. And He is your Father.
Therefore . . .
    II. YOU TOO MUST BE DIFFERENT.
       A. He expects you to reflect the family likeness
       B. In all areas of your life
       C. But not merely for the sake of being different.
Rather . . .
    III. YOU WILL BE DIFFERENT
       A. If you recognize your family relationship,
       B. If you shape your life differently from others,
       C. Who follow feelings,
       D. While you obey God's commandments.

Conclusion: The Christian life is excitingly different. No matter how you feel, obey God's commandments and you will enter into the fullness of that excitement.

Section Seven

And if you call Him Father Who impartially judges each one by his deeds, then be deeply concerned about how you behave during your residence as aliens, knowing that you weren't set free from the useless behavior patterns that were passed down from your forefathers, by the payment of a corruptible ransom like silver or gold, but with Christ's valuable blood, shed like the blood of a spotless and unblemished lamb. He was foreknown, indeed, before the foundation of a world, but at these last times He made His appearance for your sake who through Him have believed in God, Who raised Him from the dead and gave Him glory, so that your faith and hope are in God (I Pet. 1:17-21).

Christian, God is your Father; Peter has made that point in order to encourage Christians to engage in that **holy** (different) sort of **behavior** that is fitting to **children** of God. Now, more specifically, Peter begins to draw further implications from this family relationship. If you are in the family, it matters how you **live** when you find yourselves **residing** among those who don't acknowledge Him as Lord.

The family name is at stake. Therefore, he says, **be deeply concerned about how you behave.** The fact cannot be taken lightly. They must walk the paths of righteousness for His Name's sake. And this cannot be done apart from conscious thought, planning and effort (all of which are an essential part of the **concern** that God requires of them).

There are many Christians who have no concept of themselves as **aliens residing** "in the presence of the wicked" in a foreign land. The

40

sermon will have to establish the point clearly. Such Christians do and say whatever they please, heedless of the impact that their behavior and attitudes have on those who don't know God. At bottom, there is a self-centeredness behind such behavior that exhibits little concern for either God's name or the salvation of the lost.[16]

Lot was like that. He showed no concern about the arguments between his herdsmen and those of Abraham. This was a bad reflection on God's Name! They were brethren and (as Gen. 13:7 observes) the "Canaanite and the Perizzite were in the land." It was Abraham who (out of such concern) suggested splitting up and going separate ways. Later, in Sodom, when Lot warned his sons-in-law about the coming destruction, they actually thought he was kidding (Gen. 19:14). Evidently his behavior among the Sodomites gave them no indication whatever that he bore any special relationship to God.

Such matters, Peter observes, must be of deep concern (literally, "fear"; "be fearful about . . .") to the Christian. God has commanded, "Let your light shine in the presence of people so that they may see your fine deeds and glorify your Father Who is in the heavens" (Matt. 15:16). The Christian's life should be a witness to His Father in heaven. This biblical emphasis should move every believer to concern about his behavior. It is not a private matter affecting only himself; the family reputation is at stake. Every Christian daily should be aware of his alien status; this will help keep that concern alive (to reside as aliens means, literally, to "dwell beside" as aliens).

There is another point made in verse 17: the heavenly Father impartially judges each one by his deeds. This means that He plays no favorites and overlooks no sins. He will scrutinize the behavior of all His children. Each will be judged (not for salvation—that was settled at the cross—but for purposes of training and ultimate reward) on the basis of his deeds (his behavior).

The word judge refers to the judgment of a Father. It does speak of the final judgment of God among His people; but it also refers to

---

16. In chapter 3 Peter will make a point of the impact of the behavior of a husband or wife upon an unsaved spouse.

the on-going **judgment** of God by which He trains and governs the members of His family (the verb is in the present tense). And, at times when He deems it necessary (because of the disgrace it brings on His Name), that Fatherly judgment can be quite severe (cf. I Cor. 11: 28-32, 34). Let no one think that God does not judge His own; **judgment,** Peter will say later on, **begins in God's household (family,** I Pet. 4:17)!

God is **concerned** about His children's **behavior.** This command, the emphasis placed upon right behavior in this book and His **concern** to judge all, make that crystal clear. Therefore, they too should be **concerned.** This must be a large **concern** for all who are experiencing persecution and suffering.

But **concern**—if it is thought of as passive feeling alone—is not enough; it must lead to change of **behavior.** That is where many have problems. They are (indeed, have been) **concerned** about recurring life patterns that they have never been able to break, even though they know these are sinful. "Can truly significant behavioral changes be made, or are we stuck with the patterns socialized into us by our parents at an early age, as some psychiatrists teach?"

The great message of the Bible for such persons is found in verse 18. Peter affirms vigorously, "Yes! You can change! If you are His, you must come to realize (**know**) that by His death Jesus Christ has **set you free** (emancipated you) from bondage to your past sinful **patterns of behavior** that you learned from your ancestors. You are no longer slaves to the **desires** of your flesh (cf. comments on vs. 14). You are God's freedmen. He has made it possible for you to throw off past patterns of living and to replace them with new ones that please God (Rom. 6–8 has more to say about freedom from slavery to sin).[17]

Notice further that these **behavior patterns** are **useless** (cf. Eph. 4:17). That is to say, they are "empty," "vain" or "worthless." The entire book of Ecclesiastes makes clear that apart from the fear of God all is vanity (**useless**). In that powerful treatise, following the

---

17. For more on this change of patterns, replacing habits, etc., see the detailed chapters on the subject in my book, *The Christian Counselor's Manual.*

way of **desire** (cf. vs. 14) is shown to be vanity since whenever the **desire** is attained, it becomes a bubble bursting in your grasp. The very act of obtaining what one desires lessens its desirability and it becomes vain; it is no longer what you sought (or, rather, what you thought you sought). Moreover, in a world structured by God for righteous living, sinful living never works. It may for a while seem to succeed, but measured in all dimensions (remember, for instance, that Good looks at the heart when He evaluates success) and on the long term, sinful **patterns** always will be found to clash with God's reality structure. A person can no more defy God's moral laws and get away with it than he can defy His natural laws with impunity. People who jump from the Empire State Building don't break the law of gravity; they are broken by it.

And it is important (as the verse suggests) to **know** that one has been **set free.** Many follow old patterns, sensing that things are not right, but don't actually **know** that God in Christ has freed them from the grip of old habits—even from habits learned from parents in childhood. If one is unaware of this freedom, he is unlikely to avail himself of it. Christ has provided freedom *from* and freedom *to.* Not only can they overcome sinful habits, but they can learn God-pleasing ones too. The power of the Spirit to enable the believer to discover and understand God's ways in the Word and the strength He gives to walk in those ways is part of the renewal about which Peter has been speaking. In a sermon from this verse (or in a counseling session where it is appropriate) lay stress on the importance of possessing such knowledge. The member in the pew (or the counselee) ought to be asked quite pointedly, "Do you know this? Do you understand it? Do you know how to exercise this freedom to Christ's honor?" And, then, give him adequate answers.

Also, it is interesting to observe that these **useless behavior patterns were passed down from** their **forefathers.** Peter is not speaking of any sort of genetic inheritance, but of life **patterns** bequeathed to children (and to children's children—perhaps to the third and fourth generation) as part of that significant heritage of precept and example

43

that does **pass down** to later generations. Two significant questions to put are:
   (1) What sort of heritage will you pass down to your posterity?
   (2) Are you aware of these **useless patterns** that you learned from your family forebears?
Awareness of **behavior patterns** is the first step to replacing them. Listing various suggestions ("some learn to avoid responsibility, others lie their way out of tight spots, some camouflage their behavior or divert attention from it by diversionary tactics, while still others run away when the going gets tough," etc.) may help. These can be worked out more fully into fullblown illustrations if necessary.

How have we been emancipated (**freed**) from slavery to sin and the grip of its **useless behavior patterns?** Not by anything **corruptible** like the **payment** of a monetary **ransom** (such as **silver and gold;** cf. Acts 3:6, the comparison seems to be a favorite with Peter); no, not at all. **Silver and gold** are of great **value** (that's why Peter uses them in this comparison), but it took something *far more* **valuable** to redeem us and **set** us **free—Christ's** priceless **blood,** shed in sacrifice like the **blood** of a temple **lamb** slain in place of the guilty sinner as a substitute. Its **unblemished, spotless** character prefigured the sinless Savior Himself.

These truths are so well known to evangelical pastors that I shall not develop them further. It is only necessary to mention that every key word (**lamb, blood, shed, ransom**) is pregnant with O.T. background (which, incidentally, figures richly in the entire letter). In congregations where these truths are unknown they will have to be explained. A separate sermon might be preached on verses 18, 19. In other congregations, like Peter's readers who were familiar with O.T. temple ceremonies, a passing reference (like that in the passage itself) may be all that is required. But be sure that there is as much knowledge as you think. Often people have far less knowledge of such facts than we think. Terms like these can mystify if not explained to them. On the other hand, don't over explain or explain the obvious.

Interestingly, Peter again takes up the theme of **foreknowledge.**

44

It is remarkable how frequently this idea occurs in his writings and speeches. Here, by stating the fact that Christ's atoning death was **foreknown** (planned; cf. vs. 2) even **before a** single **world**[18] was created (**founded**) he brings into focus once more the amazing grace that these Christians—alive in that very time—have received. From before creation itself, this stupendous event (the focal fact in the history of the universe) has been a part of God's program. All the ages, all history moved toward it. And now—at this very time—He (the Savior of the ages) has **appeared.** "You may be suffering," in effect he says, "but you are also deeply blessed by such a privilege."

At these last times Christ **appeared** for their **sakes.** What does Peter mean by **these last times?** Literally, the original reads, "at the end of times." Clearly, Peter (writing under the inerrant guidance of the Holy Spirit) didn't intend to convey the idea that he was living at the very end of human history. Nor does it satisfy to say (as most do) that he had in view the whole N.T. era (no matter how long it might extend). That too is an unnatural explanation of the words. To what, then, does he refer? Well, he says, **Christ appeared at the end of times.** When *did* Christ in fact appear? At the close of those **times** that led up to the first advent.[19] Epochs had passed since the eternal decree went forth, and now—at the **end** of the waiting period —it had been enacted in history. Other expressions, like "the last days" (Acts 2:17) are best understood in the same way. The **end** is the **end** of those **times** that preceded and moved toward Christ's first advent.

In verse 21 Jesus Christ is viewed in His covenantal relationship to the reader. He is the crucified, **risen** and **glorified** mediatorial Son Who made a saving relationship to the Father (together with its great **hope**) possible through **faith.** Here Peter—in his way—says what John made clear when he wrote, "the one who confesses the Son, has the Father also" (I John 2:23). And both verses are an echo of

---

18. Peter's words seem to indicate that this is not the only planet that might be called a world (an organized community). However, it could as easily refer to the universe as an orderly grouping or arrangement.

19. These could be said to close with the destruction of Jerusalem in A.D. 70.

Christ's own words, "Nobody comes to the **Father** except through Me" (John 14:6; see also John 5:23). Many think they can believe in God apart from faith in Christ. But that is impossible. Christ is the *way* to God. In a message from this passage, while it should not constitute the major thrust of the sermon, somewhere this note must be sounded.

Summing up, here are the major purposes of verses 17-21 (any one of which, itself, might form the basis for a separate message):

(1) To raise concern about how a believer's behavior affects the heavenly Father's reputation among the heathen.

(2) Which, in turn, should lead to care about how to live; concern for change.

(3) To warn that God's concern for His Name will lead to impartial judgment of His children's behavior.

(4) To encourage Christians to realize that it is possible to replace long-standing sinful patterns because Christ has set us free from their grip (we are not stuck with the influence of parents, as many teach).

(5) To show that all this is because God's eternal plan of salvation has been effected by Christ.

(6) To warn that this salvation that enables believers to make behavioral change in all areas of their lives is for *believers*— those who are properly related to the Father through faith in His Son.

Clearly, that is a lot of rich material, and it is possible to emphasize one aspect of it or another (depending, perhaps, on the needs of a particular congregation or counselee). But (all other things being equal) if one emphasis must be chosen over the others, **concern for God's Name** should be selected.

Here is one way of approaching it that places the emphasis there, without neglecting the rest.

Introduction: "What difference does it make how I live? Why do you preachers get so concerned about how others live, anyway? Why not 'Live and let live'?"

Because . . .
   I. YOU ARE A CHRISTIAN
      A. If you have come to God through Christ
      B. Who gave His life as a sacrifice for His people
      C. And rose from the dead to ascend to a place of glory.
      D. Surely, you want to please Him if He has saved you.
  II. YOUR BEHAVIOR WILL HONOR OR DISHONOR
      YOUR FATHER.
      A. You live as an alien among unbelievers
      B. Who know that you belong to a different country
      C. And serve a different King (Who is your Father).
      D. They observe your behavior
      E. And honor or dishonor Him because of it.
So . . .
 III. YOU SHOULD BE CONCERNED ABOUT YOUR
      BEHAVIOR
      A. If you want to please God
      B. You will want to change
      C. By abandoning useless life patterns
      D. And adopting biblical ones.
      E. And change is possible because Christ has freed you.
 IV. GOD IS CONCERNED ABOUT YOUR BEHAVIOR
      A. Enough to command deep concern;
      B. Enough to judge you if your witness is not satisfactory.

Conclusion: Discover what patterns of behavior displeased God; find
the biblical alternatives and prayerfully seek to make the change for
His Name's sake.

Section Eight

Having cleansed yourselves by obedience to the truth you can have brotherly love without pretense; so love one another extensively from the heart, having been regenerated not by perishable seed, but by that which is imperishable—God's living and continuing Word. Do this because "all flesh is like grass and all its glory is like a flower of grass: The grass withered and the flower fell off, but the Lord's Word remains forever." Now, this is the Word that was announced to you as good news (I Pet. 1:22-25).

The next section begins with a problem (not for Peter or his readers, but for us). Peter speaks of the **cleansing** from sin that occurs in salvation as if it were the result of good works: **cleansing**, he says, was the result of **obedience to the truth.** But the difficulty is only apparent, not real.

First, notice that Peter speaks about **obedience to the truth;** he does not say **obedience** to the commandments. **Obedience to the truth** (of course) could refer to **obedience** to commandments in general, but it could also have a very specific reference. The facts show that the latter is true. The root behind the word "obey" is "to listen to" or "pay attention to." It means to obey *by heeding.* That it never lost this primary meaning is evident in modern Greek; here it still retains the idea of *obey by listenting to* as well as the simple meaning obey.

We have seen already how Peter often uses favorite words over and over (and that will be even more apparent by the conclusion of the study of this book). Now, from his use of similar terms in his letters and in his speeches in Acts, it is clear that Peter authored both (this

is one key argument against the higher critical view that Luke merely
wrote the speeches and sermons in Acts on his own as a literary de-
vice). In Acts 15:9, Peter also speaks of **cleansing,** but there he says,
"He **cleansed** their hearts *by faith.*" The two **cleansings** (I Pet./Acts)
refer to the same experience, the cleansing from sin that takes place
when a sinner believes the gospel (this is clear from the context in Acts
and from vss. 23-25 here in I Pet.[20]). **Cleansing yourselves** (lit., "your
souls") and the cleansing of *hearts* is identical. Heart (the inner life
lived before God and one's self) is equivalent to *soul* (the inner self
that gives life to the body). We may safely conclude that Peter has
the same experience and the same means of attaining cleansing in mind
in both passages. To pay attention to the truth (of the gospel; cf. vs. 25)
and to believe (or have faith) in the gospel, is not essentially different.
What Peter is saying, then, is **having cleansed yourselves by obedience
to the truth** . . . (i.e., by believing the gospel . . .).

Now the phrase describes the fulfilled condition for what follows:
you can have brotherly love without pretense. The **cleansing** from
sin that occurs when one is **sprinkled** by Christ's atoning **blood** (vs. 2)
has made genuine **love** for one's **brothers** possible. The word translated **brotherly** love, in the original is *philadelphia.* That such a concept was abroad (and had been for a long time) is apparent from the
fact that a city in Asia Minor had been given this name (Rev. 3:7ff.).
Various rulers went under that title too. Peter makes a play on this
common word and says in effect, "Now what people have talked about
can *really* take place." How could there be true brotherhood among
those who are not actually brothers? Others had spoken of such
brotherly ties, but only in the heavenly family through the new birth
could there be such a loving brotherhood among men who were not
brothers at their first birth. All other fraternal relations were but

---

20. Note especially how these words follow verse 21, in which *belief* is
stressed. The next verse (vs. 22) picks up where verse 21 ends and, referring
back to that saving *belief* in Christ that he has just described, he now says,
Having cleansed . . . , etc. This **obedience to the truth,** therefore, is but another way of speaking about *heeding* the gospel call and command to believe; it
is trusting in the truth about Christ's sacrificial death and bodily resurrection
(cf. footnote on 2:8).

talk, a shame; mere **pretense** (lit., hypocrisy). Christian counselees who deny the possibility of loving another Christian can be faced with this passage. "Either it is possible," they may be told, "or you deny your own salvation. Christ cleansed us for this purpose." Again, Peter speaks of Christ's **salvation setting** us **free** for new experiences in life. Our **cleansing** was to enable us to do new things, such as loving others as never before. So, then, he continues, **love one another extensivly (to the fullest extent) from the heart**. It is worth noting that Peter changes the word **love** from *phileo* to *agapao*. Indeed, Peter is saying that Christ not only made **brotherly friendship** (*philia*) possible, but even **love** that gives (*agape*). And not only is **love** (over against true **friendship**) possible, but love to the fullest **(love extensively)**. Such love is far-reaching in its implications (examples of love that extends itself, culminating in Christ's **love,** of course, might be given; cf. Rom. 8:38, 39; I Cor. 13). And this **love** that we are discussing is not a sham; it is **love from the heart** (i.e., genuine.[21]).

And this transformation was the work of God, Who gave us a new life (**regenerated** us[22]). Our new life came through no **perishable** physical **seed** (or sperm) as our first life did (cf. I John 3:9 for a similar usage). Rather, we were **regenerated through** (*dia*) God's **imperishable Word** that (contrary to what happens to much **perishable seed**) is **living** and also **continuing** (it **remains**). This **Word** is the **good news;** the gospel message **announced** by the apostles (vs. 12). In this regard, cf. especially Acts 10:36. Peter's comment about the *spora* (**seed**) continuing reminds him of its more common usage and, in particular, of Isaiah 40:6-8, in which the transient nature of human life is contrasted with God's enduring Word (vss. 24, 25).

The words "all flesh" are a Hebraism for "every person" (cf.

---

21. Heart in the Scriptures never means "feelings," as it does in our culture (influenced by Roman thought). Rather heart is always contrasted with *outer things* like lips or the mouth (cf. Matt. 12:34; 15:8). It is *never* contrasted with the head (contrast our expression, heart knowledge/head knowledge).

22. Peter, let it be noted carefully, does not use the word regeneration in its more theological sense (as *quickening* or *life-giving*) but in a broader sense to indicate an entire change of life.

Gen. 8:17; 9:11, 15. 16; and understood clearly by Jews in N.T. times: Acts 2:17). The perishable nature of human life since the fall is aptly portrayed by Isaiah as grass. In contrast, the gospel is eternal (Rev. 14:6).

If, then, the Christian possesses a new capability for genuine **love** as the consequence of his renewal, making it possible through **cleansing,** he must take advantage of that fact and learn to **love** other Christians to the **fullest extent.** This is the major thrust of the section under consideration.

This interlude (vss. 22-25) and others like it, in which Peter digresses somewhat from the main thread of his discussion (cf., for instance, 1:19-21; 2:4-7, 9, 10, etc.) is not unintentional; it is part of Peter's technique. His concern is to *remind* the readers of the basic truths of their faith (cf. II Pet. 1:12; 3:1). Whenever appropriate, therefore Peter issues such reminders.

Reminders are needed (and serve a valuable purpose) in times of trouble and persecution. Counselors should take this fact to heart and use more reminders than they often do. Reminders of

(1) what God has done, and

(2) what He promises to do

together with a comparison of these facts with the transitory nature of

(1) present troubles (vs. 6), and

(2) present glories (vs. 24, the *best* this life has to offer of fame, power, wealth, etc.)

help to put matters into perspective. One of the principal temptations for suffering persons is the temptation to become involved (and totally caught up in) the immediate. This is easy to do because the immediate is so vivid; suffering is painful! But to do so is a sure way to fail to honor God in the suffering. He will fail because the lack of depth and perspective in his view of the circumstances causes thoughts of God and His holy purposes to fade. In the end, he views trial in much the same way that an unsaved person does. So what Peter is doing is to fight the tendency to pagan thinking by some very heavy reminders. These reminders are so prominent in his writings that a series of sermons based entirely upon them might be preached. The operative verb in the section is *agapao,* "to **love** (vs. 22). Around it, the whole section revolves. The sermon, then, should be about **love** for one's brothers. It might take a form like this:

Introduction: There is so much that falsely claims to be brotherly love (example). There are so many abortive attempts to achieve such love (examples). But they all fail (examples). Is it possible? Yes; if you . . .

   I. BELONG TO GOD'S FAMILY, YOU CAN LOVE

      A. By receiving a new life (regeneration)
      B. Through obedience to the truth (faith in the gospel)
      C. Which was announced to you
      D. And continues forever.

  II. AND YOU CAN LOVE GENUINELY

      A. Other love is in pretense only.
      B. True brotherly love is
         1. from the heart (i.e., genuine) and is
         2. *agape* love (i.e., giving); not *philia* only.
      C. And this love can be extensive enough
         1. To cover a multitude of sins (4:8),
         2. To reach out to others, far beyond what pagans do.

Conclusion: This love (unlike things purely human) lasts, like the gospel that made it possible. Invest yourself in what is permanent.

CHAPTER TWO

Section Nine

Therefore, having put off all malice, and all pretense and hypocritical ways, and envious attitudes, and all evil speaking about others, like newborn babies, crave pure spiritual milk so that by it you may grow toward salvation, since "you have tasted that the Lord is good" (I Pet. 2:1-3).

The chapter headings in the Bible were added hundreds of years after its writing. While they are a convenience, they are fallible, often placed inappropriately and frequently break into the flow of thought. Such is the case here (why not, from time to time, make a point of this to your people to clue them in on the need to read through such headings in order to understand a given passage).

A **therefore** in verse 1 signals the approach of an exhortation that is the conclusion to an argument or discussion that has preceded (Tell your people to ask always, "What is the 'therefore' there for?"). In this section a dependent clause (vs. 1) is followed by the exhortation proper (vs. 2) which, in turn, is followed by a biblical quotation that provides a reason.

Having disposed of (**put off**[1]) those things that hinder growth in Christian living, Peter says, make room for (indeed, **crave**) that which promotes it. The **therefore** connects this exhortation with the preceding discussion, in which Peter reminded his readers that they have been renewed by **regeneration** to newness of life. This life, into which

---

1. Cf. Rom. 13:12; Col. 3:5ff.; Eph. 4:22, where it is plain that, in Christ, the old way of life has been put off. The believer, therefore, must count himself rid of all the old ways in Him. Yet, in these passages, he also is exhorted (as here in I Peter) to become (in everyday life) what he already is (in Christ).

they have entered, and the powers that they have begun to experience, are the result of faith in the good news about Christ's death and resurrection. This new life now makes it possible to abandon the old sinful ways of the former life, so that one may **put off** such things as

> **malice** (badness, viciousness, a desire to harm others),
> **imposture** (guile; trickery; lit., catching with bait),
> **hypocritical ways** (misrepresenting true intentions, attitudes, etc.),
> **envious attitudes** (displeasure over another's good fortune; Matt. 27:18), and
> **all** (every sort of) **evil speaking about others**[2] (especially behind their backs).

Every counselor should familiarize himself with these terms; they describe well much of what he must confront in his counselees. Early in every series of counseling sessions, he should take an inventory of the counselee based on this verse to see what sort of problems he will find it necessary to deal with.

Many of the difficulties encountered in counseling stem from one or more of these negative qualities. New converts, as well as counselees in general, might profit greatly from a discussion of the need to eliminate these factors from their new lives in Christ.

Again, counselors must see to it that all such behavior and any such attitudes are discouraged in counseling sessions. They may be neither encouraged (feeling-oriented approaches often encourage sinful behavior) nor permitted ("This will be the one hour in the week when you will act like Christians").[3] Perhaps the place where counselors sin most greatly is in allowing counselees to **speak negatively about others** behind their backs. All such attempts—as well as sinful expressions of sinful attitudes in bad language—must be prohibited. If the counselee persists (after warning) he must be rebuked in love. If he continues, he may need to be dismissed from counseling tempo-

---

2. The verbal form is found later in this chapter (2:12). The word refers, literally, to "speaking another down"; cf. especially James 4:11.

3. For more on this, see my book, *Matters of Concern for Christian Counselor*, pp. 77ff.

rarily until he repents, or (in the event that no repentance is forth-coming) church discipline (in rare cases) may need to be instituted. In preaching, examples of behavior described by each word will help to clarify and fix their meaning for the congregation.

Now, in the place of all these things that must be disposed of, Peter urges the believer to **crave** (long or yearn for) **pure** (unmixed, unadulterated[4]) **milk** as **newborn babies** do so that they **may** be nour-ished and **grow** toward the glorification and perfection that the full realization of their **salvation** will bring at death (or at Christ's return).

This **craving** for God's **pure milk** (truth) should develop from **tasting** how **good** the **Lord** is. The **baby** gets a **taste** of milk and thereafter wants it as often as he needs it. The Christian must de-velop a **taste** (leading to a strong desire—in contrast to the worldly desires condemned throughout this letter) for what is **good** for him and will help him to **grow** holy. Thus, God requires a change of eat-ing habits. The wicked poisons—so often sugar-coated to make them seem palatable—listed in verse 1 must be rejected and replaced by the healthy **milk** of verse 2 (cf. Ps. 34:8).

But this **milk** must not be contaminated. Two major points are made: (1) a desire for God's truth must be cultivated; (2) God's truth must not be contaminated by mixture with error. To keep the truth pure and wholesome, it must be pasteurized; all of the toxins of verse 1 that could make it dangerous must be eliminated. Unknow-ingly, many Christians go on day after day drinking poisonous sub-stitutes for the real thing. Only by careful study of the Bible can such admixtures be discovered (cf. Acts 17:11. If Paul commended check-ing up on what he said, then it is vital to do the same for every other teacher. It is important to guide your people to make Scrip-ture their final standard—not any teacher or their own personal experience).

---

4. The devil uses the world to contaminate God's truth by its eclectic ways. Christians must become alert to all such tendencies to mix error with God's truth. Peter urges a diet of pure, undiluted, uncontaminated spiritual milk. For a striking example of such contamination, see my book, *The Power of Error.*

Any mixture of God's truth and God's ways with the sinful attitudes and practices detailed in verse 1 must be avoided. The mixture may come from the counselee's or the listener's desire to hold on to sinful patterns. But true Christians—those who have genuinely **tasted** the Lord's **goodness** and discovered for themselves how **good** it is—will more and more hunger and thirst for *pure* **milk**. A person, purporting to be a Christian, who has never yearned for God's truth or who has never shown **growth** in his life, is not a genuine Christian. He could no more be God's child than a baby could be alive and refrain from crying for **milk**. But the problem here is not a false profession of faith (Peter assumes the genuineness of their faith); rather, the problem (so prevalent today) is that Christians can be swindled. Under the label of **pure milk** every sort of mixture is offered on the supermarket shelf. Peter wants his readers to be sure that what they drink will promote, rather than stunt, Christian **growth.**

The use of the figure of speech here (**milk**), unlike its use in I Corinthians 3:1 and Hebrews 5:12, does not convey the idea of spiritual immaturity. There is no condemnation of desiring **milk** (rather than solid food), but, on the contrary, a strong plea to do so. The points that Peter wishes to make differ; that is why his use of the figure differs too. Peter wants, rather, to emphasize the importance of (1) developing a desire (**craving**) for God's truth over against his former desires for the devil's lies, and (2) the need to be aware that not all that goes for milk is **pure** (much has been adulterated).

Peter wants his readers to **grow** toward **salvation.** Here, and in II Peter 3:18, **growth** is said to depend upon the Lord's help. He, by giving knowledge of Christ (**pure milk**), promotes Christian growth. This knowledge, the contexts show, is not merely knowledge *about* (truth known abstractly), but knowledge *of* (truth known experientially). Growth comes to those who **put off** the sorts of sinful patterns mentioned in verse 1 and who (by learning God's will) find those patterns that please God. These patterns are all found in the Scriptures as biblical alternatives.

When Peter calls this **pure milk** of God's truth, *spiritual* **milk** (as opposed to literal; see Moulton and Milligan), he is thinking of milk that provides **spiritual** nourishment. Here, as in 3:21, where Peter distinguishes between literal and non-literal baptism, he wants to make sure that his readers clearly understand that he is using a figure of speech.

To **taste** is to know by experience and to discover for one's self. Peter says, since you have accepted God's invitation to **taste and see** (Ps. 34:8) by personal faith in Jesus Christ, you should *know* that the **pure milk** of God's truth is **good** and necessary for your **growth.**

There is a sermon here on hungering and thirsting for righteousness, with a twist: not all that purports to be milk is pure. One way to develop this purpose follows:[5]

Introduction: Most of us eat a lot of junk food that is not really nutritional, and may even be harmful. Some of the additives mixed into our foods also have been proven poisonous. We must be careful what we eat. Many of us need a change of diet. The same is true spiritually. As unbelievers, we consumed error daily that was poisoning us. Now that we have come to Christ, we must change our eating habits.

    I. YOU HAVE TASTED GOD'S TRUTH
        A. When you trusted in Christ as your Savior from sin
        B. And He saved you!
        C. So, you know that He is good
        D. And provides good things for your spiritual nourishment.
So . . .
    II. YOU MUST DEVELOP AN APPETITE FOR GOD'S TRUTH
        A. Like a newborn baby that craves milk,
        B. By remembering the good things you've already tasted,

---

5. By the way, these outlines are but the bare bones. Exact wording, and in particular examples (I have only mentioned *some* of the places where these are required), must be added.

C. By studying His menu for you (the Scriptures).
III. YOU MUST BE SURE THAT YOU DRINK PURE MILK
    A. Satan loves to contaminate the believer's food.
       (Develop examples as subpoints)
    B. Christians themselves do so by wanting to hold on to sinful practices (vs. 1).
    C. The Scriptures alone can tell you what is pure truth and what is poisonous error.
IV. YOU WILL GROW FROM GOD'S TRUTH
    A. Growth is important; God desires it.
    B. God wants you to make progress throughout your life (toward salvation).

Conclusion: So, crave pure milk! Don't adulterate it in any way.

Section Ten

As you come to Him, a living Stone (on the one hand rejected by men, but on the other hand, to God choice and valuable), like living stones, you yourselves are being built into a spiritual house for a holy priesthood to offer spiritual sacrifices acceptable to God through Jesus Christ. Scripture says: "See, I am laying in Zion a choice Stone, a valuable Cornerstone; and whoever believes on Him will never be put to shame." So to believers He is of value, but to unbelievers "the very Stone that the builders disapproved of has become the Head of the corner," and, "a Stone to stumble over, a Rock to trip over." They stumble, as indeed they were appointed to, because they are disobedient to the Word (I Pet. 2:4-8).

It is interesting (and instructive) to note how naturally the N.T. writers interpret O.T. passages that speak about Jehovah (the covenant or salvation title for God) to Jesus Christ. And it is done without any fanfare whatsoever. That is what Peter does when in verse 4 he refers back to verse 3 (a quotation from Ps. 34:8) and writes: **As you come to Him (Christ) a living Stone. . . .** This **coming** is the **coming** of faith in response to the invitation **taste and see . . .** , and subsequent comings in faith to praise and thank Him for His salvation and the many benefits that it includes.

As Peter begins to develop the thought of **tasting,** he abruptly switches the metaphor to one that grows out of a cluster of O.T. passages that come to mind (Gen. 49:24; Isa. 8:14; 28:16, etc.), all having to do with the **Stone.** The Lord Jesus is the **Stone** to which they come. But like the **living hope** (1:3) and the **living Word** (1:23), so this **Stone** is the **living Stone.** A stone is usually thought of as the epitome of the inanimate (that idea lay behind Christ's remarkable words in Luke 19:40). By adding the word **living,** Peter makes it clear that the **Stone** is a Person;[6] indeed, it is the Lord Himself! Why Peter switches to this figure is not immediately apparent. The **Stone** passage (Isa. 8:14) is frequently used in the N.T. by Christ and the apostles and Peter himself (Acts 4:11).

When we **come** to Christ as the **Stone,** we **come** to Him as a **foundation** for our lives (vs. 6), a very deep concept best left for full development in a separate sermon at a later time when not preaching through the book (work this out fully by contrasting faulty human foundations).

These same persons (here, primarily Jews; cf. Matt. 21:42, 43) who build their lives on sand, **reject** Him. These poor **builders** fail to see Him as the only solid and secure foundation for human existence. Yet to **God** the Father He is the most **choice** and **valuable Stone** of all (cf. Isa. 28:16). **God's** judgment leads to an evaluation of Christ that diametrically opposes theirs. They say, "This stone is of no use to us," and cast it aside. Then, they attempt to build on some other foundation. But as they try to construct life on a different foundation, they discover that they are not really rid of that **Stone** at all—they are continually **stumbling** and **tripping** over it.[7] **He** is always there; they can never get away from Him (cf. Ps. 139); at the most unexpected times they stumble over Him. Christ divides; some **build** on Him, others **stumble** over Him. As a **rock** can be the occasion for either response, so is He among men. And the dividing factor is **belief:** they **stumble** because they are **disobedient** to the **Word** (they **reject** the **gospel**).[8] What is involved in this **stumbling** perhaps is best understood by a careful exegesis of Isaiah 8:14, 15 (see E. J. Young's

---

6. Cf. Paul's use of *"living* . . . sacrifice"* in Romans 12:1.
7. Picture the stone that was rejected and cast aside lying on the construction site where it was thrown; grass grows up around it. As they go about their work, from time to time the builders trip and fall over it (some may even be severely injured). That is the image of the stone of stumbling (or the stumbling block).
8. Note, once again, how disobedience to the Word (the gospel message) is contrasted with belief. The one is set over against the other as its opposite.

Commentary on Isaiah in the *New International Commentary* series).
The idea of **stumbling** at the **Word** comes (as do many of the
apostles' figures of speech) from Christ's own usage (cf. Matt.
5:12; Mark 14:17; see also John 6:60). See also Paul's discussion of Israel's stumbling in Romans 11:9-11, in which tripping so as to fall
means utter and total rejection.

To **God**, the Father, Christ is a **valuable rock** that He has **chosen**
to be the church's **Cornerstone**. Anyone who is a part of that church
will build his life on Him. Christ binds the building together at the
foundation, thus performing a basic, honorable and fundamental
function. The chief (**head**) **cornerstone** is the primary foundation
stone. He is, then, a **choice Stone;** the One Whom God has chosen
to honor this way. Woe to those **disobedient** construction workers
who **reject** the Master's Builder's judgment! Because they did, God
Himself **laid** this **Stone** in **Zion**. To reject Jesus Christ is to reject
God Himself. The **Stone laid in Zion** by God is placed there because
that's where Christ's sacrifice was made, where His resurrection took
place, and where Pentecost (Acts 2) occurred. So the law, beginning at Jerusalem, went forth from **Zion** (cf. Isa. 2:3; Ps. 110:2).

What now of **believers?** People in general (as well as Israel in
general) **reject** and **stumble** over Christ. God highly **values** Him.
True believers will take their stand with God, accept His evaluation
of the situation (His philosophy of history, etc.), and also will prize
Him (vs. 7). In Him they have absolute assurance that they will
never (this is a very strong negative in the Greek; *ou me*) **be put to
shame** (vs. 6), which is another way of saying that in spite of how
things look during trial and tribulation—in which Christ is all but
universally **rejected**—He will *never* let them down. They will not be
disappointed in their hope. **Value** Him; **trust** and **obey** Him; He is
the trustworthy one—as solid as a rock! All others—family, friends,
Christians, preachers—at one time or another will let us down. The
one who depends on Christ **will *never* be ashamed.**

Moreover, Jesus Christ is the One through Whom **believers** themselves have become **living stones** in God's temple (vs. 5). He is the
One by Whom they have been admitted into the church. God is

building them, one by one, into His church; each becomes a **valued block** in that edifice. This **building**—His temple—is to house a **holy priesthood.** (Now the imagery shifts momentarily from believers as **living stones** to believers as **holy priests** officiating in the temple. Of course, it is very simple, when using imagery, to leap from one concept to another as the latter is suggested by the former. In explaining this passage when preaching, it might be important to note the fact since there are so many Christians who fail to understand the elasticity of imagery and are confused by it.)

This **priesthood** of all believers is to be **holy** (different; cf. the discussion of the word **holy** in 1:15, 16). One difference is that it is a **royal** or **kingly priesthood** (cf. discussion of vs. 9; see also Rev. 1:6). The task of this **priesthood** is to **offer spiritual** (not literal) **sacrifices.** These **sacrifices** are not bloody ones; Christ's shed blood put an end to all expiation by blood once for all. Calvary was the final blood **sacrifice,** after which Jesus (unlike O.T. priests) sat down, because His work was complete. In this respect the **priesthood** was different too (cf. Heb. 9, 10). The **sacrifices** offered to God by this new and different **priesthood** that He has set apart for Himself are **sacrifices** of praise and thanksgiving (cf. Heb. 13:15). And they are **spiritual.** That is to say, the Holy Spirit motivates the **believer-priest** to offer them and even modifies them to make them a sweet-smelling savor to God (cf. Rom. 8:26, 27). They are **offered** in Christ's Name, a fact that gives them further **acceptability.** (We have no access to the Father except through the Son. Fundamentally, to pray in Christ's Name is to acknowledge that fact.) Even praise and thanksgiving must be offered **through Jesus Christ,** the One Who has made it possible to become **priests** in God's temple.

But the **unbeliever stumbles** over the **Stone.** That means that he has neither a part in the **building** (as a **living stone**) nor in the **priesthood.** Both are **holy** (special, different, set apart from the rest to God). And, according to verse 8, **unbelievers** were **appointed** to **stumble.** The word **appointed** is, literally, "to place or set or ordain." It was used regularly of drawing up official documents like bonds or wills (see Moulton and Milligan). It also was used (vs. 6) of God

laying (setting, placing, appointing) His **Stone** in **Zion.** The concept of appointment to destruction is not an isolated one (cf. Luke 2:34; Jude 4). God's eternal purpose (**appointment**) is carried out through man's responsible action (**disobedience**). See further comments on I Peter 1:2.

These five verses at first may seem difficult to pull together. But if comments about the **building** are accorded the subsidiary place that this theme occupied in this passage (perhaps a separate sermon about the building would do), then a unity around the evaluation of the **Stone** may be seen.

Suffering Christians, persecuted and driven forth as refugees, would be well aware of the fact that those in power reject the **Stone** and His followers. Here, Peter anticipates some of the problems that this fact poses, and in the light of such potential difficulties sweeps them all aside by calling for a different evaluation of Him. How can you, whom He has made fellow-**stones** in God's temple, do any less? The Jews (in general) have **rejected** Him, but you **believing** Jews know that God has given Him the most important and prominent place in the church. He prizes Him as **choice** and **valuable.** You must do the same.

Because the **builders rejected** God's **choice Stone,** that same **Stone** has become an occasion for **stumbling** to them. Ultimately, those who continue in **disobedience** and refuse to heed the command to repent and to **believe** the gospel, will fall utterly (it will mean that at the final judgment they will be sent eternally to hell). According to God's purposes (nothing happens but what He **ordains**), they will suffer not those temporal pains and agonies with which they are now afflicting the church, but the everlasting pangs of hell. And though, in God's providence it all happens according to His decree, because their responsible acts are the means he has chosen for carrying out that decree, they will have no reason for complaint (they **rejected** Christ, would not **believe** the gospel, **disobeyed** the message).

Introduction: Sometimes it seems like no one else believes in Christ; you are all alone. It can be very discouraging (if we allow it) to see how much disbelief and disobedience there are. Has your praise for Christ slackened? At such times you need to remember that . . .

I. CHRIST IS YOUR FOUNDATION STONE
    A. A valuable Stone, chosen by God Himself
    B. As the foundation for your life
    C. And the Cornerstone of His church
    D. Which is the temple in which you are priests
    E. Not to offer atoning sacrifices of blood, but
    F. To offer sacrifices of praise and thanksgiving.

II. THOUGH JEWISH BUILDERS REJECTED GOD'S STONE
    A. Through unbelief and disobedience
    B. To the good news about Christ's death and resurrection
    C. So God has made Him a Stone of stumbling
    D. Over which they will ultimately trip into hell
    E. If they remain in unbelief.

III. YOU MUST VALUE HIM HIGHLY
    A. Come to Him (don't turn away in trial)
    B. As to One Whom you prize
    C. As a priest bringing thanksgiving and praise
    D. And remember, in all your hopes He will never let you down
    E. Unlike these builders, you will never fall utterly or be ashamed.

Conclusion: Prize Him and you will praise Him!

Section Eleven

But you have become a chosen race, a kingly priesthood, a holy nation, a people who belong to Someone, so that you may declare the virtues of the One Who called you out of darkness into His amazing light. At one time you were not a people, but now are God's people; you were without mercy, but now you have been shown mercy (I Pet. 2:9-10).

The Jewish **builders rejected** Christ, but that didn't stop God *Himself* from **laying** His **choice Stone** in **Zion**. Indeed, in spite of them, He founded and built His church. Christ predicted all this in a parable that He concluded with these words:

And Jesus said to them, "Didn't you ever read in the Scriptures: 'The same Stone that the builders rejected has become the Head of the corner; this has happend because of the Lord and it is astonishing in our eyes'? So then I tell you that God's empire will be taken away from you and will be given to a nation who will produce its fruit" (Matt. 21:42, 43).

Referring to Hosea 2:23, in confirmation of the amazing things said about her, the N.T. church, that is composed of converted Jews and Gentiles,[9] **was not a people** (vs. 10); but now in fulfillment of all the O.T. prophecies concerning Israel (Peter says), God has constituted her as **His people** instead of the unbelieving builders. **Mercy** had been extended to them in Christ; they *deserved* nothing and had *known* nothing of such saving mercy in the past. This formation of a new **people** of God, like the older people, was strictly the result of

---

9. Cf. Romans 9:26, where Paul quotes the same prophecy and applies it to Gentiles. It is clear, from this double use, that the prophecy refers to the N.T. church in general.

God's **mercy;** all was of grace: the initiative was taken by God, the salvation was accomplished by God, and it was applied to individuals by God.

The word **people** means "natives" (Moulton and Milligan) or "folk." It has connotations of unity in warmth. It is clear that what God has constituted is a **people** who are His, on whom He has set His love and toward whom He has shown mercy in Christ.

Peter reminds his readers that they are not alone. There is a unity with other believers. Christians are not autonomous units; the social need in man is met by Christ through His **people.** That means they do not have to face trials and sorrows alone; the burdens (and joys) of one are the burdens (and joys) of all. A **people** is a group of persons who are bound together by common sympathies and interests. These ties arise out of the great truths that they hold in common—truths that have brought about kinship as a part of God's family. Travelling in all parts of the world, I have met Christians of every description, but our common bond as the **people of God** transcends the differences. There is a mutual recognition of that unity in Christ that both parties sense: "You're one of my **people!**" Recognition of this unity is important always, but especially in times of persecution. It is good to know that there are *others that God has provided* to share in sorrows.

In preaching or counseling from this verse, it might be important to ask, "Have you availed yourself of this provision? Do you think of yourself as having roots; as a part of a people? Are the believers you know 'your folk'?" There are many Christians who through embarrassment (or other forms of pride[10]) suffer alone. They have lost (or never properly known) the joys of having kinfolk in Christ to whom they may turn in a crisis or need. It is necessary, in all we do as pastors, to cultivate the sense of belonging to **God's people.** In this fractured society in which we live, many of the problems people are experiencing come from their lack of ties. They are simply adrift. **Resident aliens** (cf. vs. 11), like these Christians to whom Peter was

10. If one were not overly concerned about himself, he would experience no embarrassment or shyness.

writing, know that there are no permanent earthly ties upon which to depend. But this heavenly **people,** nomadic though it may be (cf. Heb. 11), is lasting. **God's people** will continue; their roots are in heaven.

Peter is careful to stress that the formation of this **people** is not their own doing; they were constituted a **people** strictly by God's **mercy.** In His goodness, God has done for them all the wonderful things noted in verse 9. But "remember," he says, "it is all of **mercy.**" He wants us to treat our privileges as such. We must take nothing for granted (which means, we must not take *God* for granted).

It is necessary, from time to time, to shake up a trial-weary congregation (or counselee) to its rights, privileges and opportunities by reemphasizing its advantages in Christ. As we consider verse 9, keep that fact in mind and think about how you (in a sermon or counseling session) could use the verse to encourage Christians to new zeal and effort.

In verse 9 four great facts are stated about the New Testament church. Peter says, you have become:

(1) **A chosen race** (cf. Isa. 43:20),

(2) **A kingly priesthood** (cf. Ex. 19:6; Rev. 1:6; 5:10; 20:6),

(3) **A holy nation** (cf. Ex. 19:6), and

(4) **A people who belong to Someone** (cf. Isa. 43:20b; Ex. 19: 5; 26:18; Deut. 7:6; 14:2; Mal. 3:17; Tit. 2:14).

The words used to describe the standing, functions and privileges of the New Testament church all have their origin in the description of the Old Testament church (see Scripture references above). Obviously, Peter wanted to stress the continuity between the two. His (largely) Jewish Christian readers would immediately understand this intention. And, in addition, he wanted to make clear that the New Testament church *entirely* superseded the Old Testament church —all of its prerogatives had been transferred to it. The **stumbling** of the old **builders** led to their loss of status as a **people** of **God.** In no sense, therefore, is it correct to speak of unbelieving Jews today as God's people or the chosen people. Those titles, as Peter shows, belong exclusively to the New Testament church. Paul affirms this too, of course, when he insists that the true Israel and the true seed of Abraham is those Jews and Gentiles who have faith in Christ (cf. Gal. 4:29; Rom. 4:11, 12, 16).

Peter once again affirms the love that God expressed toward the church when he writes **you have become a chosen race.** This choice was a determination to set His love on His people (cf. Eph. 1:4, 5). This was a choice in love. When Jesus told the apostles, "You didn't choose Me; rather I chose you" (John 15:16), He wanted to remind them that their place in the church was the result of loving grace; there was no room for pride.

On the other hand, there is a place for pride—in God. A balance must be struck. To be **chosen** by God is to become a part of a new **race** of men; the new Israel that He loved and brought into being. This is a great privilege. The word **chosen,** at once, removes all boasting and yet establishes a dignity of heredity that enables a **chosen** one to point to God as the Father of his **race.** The Jews (wrongly) looked to Abraham as the father of Israel. But the true Father of (spiritual) Israel[11] was God Himself. Thus, the **chosen race** is the only race that rightly may take pride in its origins, since God Himself is the Originator; the Great Ancestor. But whenever the shift from pride in God to pride in the race itself occurs, that leads to disaster (cf. the exchange in John 6, esp. vss. 33-44; it is possible to have pride in human ancestry and not realize that one's true father is the devil).

When speaking of His **people** as **chosen** God Himself makes the point that this excludes all human merit and pride. Neither old nor new Israel merited this free, loving choice: cf. Deuteronomy 7:6-8 (a good passage to read aloud to the congregation, especially in the Berkeley Version. The chosen people is a race that was adopted by the great God of creation; in that God alone one can boast.

The joy and thanksgiving and humility and encouragement arising from a comprehension and appreciation of all this is important for suffering saints. Peter knew that it was necessary for a persecuted

---

11. Cf. Romans 9:6, 8; there was an Israel within Israel.

church, ragged and torn as it may be outwardly, to see itself as God sees it. This new light, he believed, could best be thrown upon the circumstances by stating the facts succinctly in one sentence, so that his readers could comprehend and contemplate them. It would not be unwise to encourage modern day Christians to turn to this passage frequently to do the same.

You might think that to say one belongs to a **chosen race,** of which God is both Chooser and Ancestor, would be enough. But Peter has only begun. To this he adds, **you are . . . a kingly priesthood.** I shall not discuss the concept of a spiritual **priesthood** further (see comments on vs. 5). At this point, the notion of a *kingly* **priesthood** should be noted. Unlike the O.T. **priesthood,** in which priestly functions were limited almost entirely to Levi's descendants, in the New Testament church all believers are priests. Their function, as we have seen (cf. vs. 5), is to **offer sacrifices of** praise and thanksgiving through the Holy Spirit. And they do so *as kings!* The church is a **people,** all of whom are both **priests** and **kings** (cf. Rev. 1:6; 20:6). Like their Lord, they bear both titles and engage in both functions.[12]

Now, to view these poor suffering outcasts to whom Peter was writing, no one would ever suspect them of being *kings.* **Kings** indeed! How could refugees, driven out by persecution, make good on that claim? The idea—to worldly eyes—was absurd.[13] But they can live in a **kingly** way in this world, show a **kingly** bearing before their persecutors as their Lord (a **King** also) did when no one, outwardly, could see other evidences of His kingship. Like **kings** of old, going forth to war, they can fight spiritual battles, defeating sin and Satan.[14] When down and discouraged, the believer may recall Peter's

---

12. And though he does not single it out in exactly the same way, Peter also recognizes their prophetic function: **so that you may declare the virtues. . . .** Thus, Christians are prophets, priests and kings!

13. In C. S. Lewis' Narnia stories a similar idea is developed. There mere children (as the world sees them) become kings and queens fighting for kingdoms in the spiritual world.

14. For a discussion of Christ's battle orders, see my book, *How to Overcome Evil.*

reminder of who he is—a **king!** Taking heart from this, he can rise from his ashes and go out in Christ's power to triumph! Counselees —many of whom are defeated—need just such a reminder. Can one be **kingly** in suffering and pain? Christ was **King** supremely on Calvary.[15]

Peter doesn't leave it that way either; he goes on to declare, **you are . . . a holy nation.** A band of scattered refugees, a nation! laughable? Again, one who can see with nothing more than an unconverted eye snickers at the thought. But what constitutes a **nation?** A central government, with laws and functions, governed by a ruler, and a people who bear allegiance to that government. Christ, His Book, His people and His organized church are that **holy nation!**

Now Christ's **nation** is **holy** (see the discussion of this term under 1:15, 16). **Holy** means different, unique. Part of that difference surfaced when Christ told Pilate, "My kingdom is not from this world" (John 18:36). The worldwide kingdom (or empire, since Christ is King of kings and Lord of lords; Rev. 19:16) of Jesus Christ is **a nation** within nations; an empire of people from all peoples; some out of "every tribe and tongue and people and nation" (Rev. 5:9). It demands primary allegiance and, yet, thereby makes its citizens even better citizens of the temporal governments to which they also are subject (cf. esp. 2:13-16). This dual citizenship is also unique. Moreover, the **nation** of God's people is unique because its seat of authority is in heaven (it is called the Kingdom—or Empire—from the Heavens). And all its conquests are made by the sword of the Word (Rev. 19:11-16). Its King is Jesus Christ, the God-man. It was He Who said of this worldwide empire, "All authority is given to Me in heaven and on earth" (Matt. 28:18). And on the basis of that claim He told His church to recruit disciples from all over the world.

Finally, Peter calls the church **a people who belong to Someone.** They are a **people** (see earlier comments on vs. 10) who belong to God as His private property. God called them to make them His peculiar treasure, devoted exclusively to Him (cf. Ex. 19:5). Because

---

15. One of the thieves even recognized it and asked to be remembered when He came into His kingdom.

we are Jehovah's, He cares for us. He takes care of His possessions. No one can steal His property or ultimately harm it; He guards and protects what belongs to Him. These words of Peter are good news to suffering saints. Truly understood, such a reminder is (to use a favorite Petrine word) valuable.

But Peter wrote all of these things not only to comfort and encourage in suffering. That is important; he wanted to confirm their faith. They must *trust;* but they must also *obey.* So, he goes on to point out that God constituted His church of persons with all these titles and the privileges they bestow in order that they also may exercise the duties that each title implies, one of which is **to declare the virtues of the One Who called** them **out of darkness into His amazing light.** All these privileges have this evangelistic end in view.

The excellencies (or virtues) of God that the church must declare among the heathen (by word and deed) are reflected in the amazing things that He has done for His people described by the four titles we have just discussed. Such a call (to be **a chosen race, a kingly priesthood, a holy nation and a people who belong to Someone**), he says, is nothing less than a summons to leave the utter **darkness** of heathenism in which they were living, to dwell in the realms of blazing, **amazing light** (cf. I Pet. 5:10; Col. 1:13; Eph. 5:8-14; Isa. 9:2; 60:1-3).

Here is one way to outline it all:

Introduction: Christian, are you discouraged, careworn, defeated by sin? Has the struggle with sin got you down? Evidently you have forgotten who you are! Listen to this (read vss. 9, 10).

I. YOU HAVE BEEN GREATLY HONORED BY GOD
   A. Who made you part of His chosen race,
   B. A kingly priesthood,
   C. A holy nation and
   D. A people who belong to Somebody!
   E. This is tantamount to saying you have come from utter darkness

F. Into amazing light.
II. YOU HAVE RECEIVED ALL THIS IN MERCY
   A. Not because of who or what you were—
   B. You weren't even a people and
   C. You knew nothing of such mercy;
   D. But God set His love on you in Christ
   E. And through His death and resurrection called you to Himself.
III. BUT YOU WERE CHOSEN FOR A PURPOSE
   A. To declare His virtues to the heathen—
   B. What He is,
   C. What He has done,
   D. What He has promised—
   E. By your words and works.

Conclusion: Wake up! Thank Him! Look and live like what you *really* are!

Section Twelve

Dear friends, as resident aliens and refugees, I urge you to keep at a safe distance from the fleshly desires that are poised against your soul like an expeditionary force, having good behavior among the Gentiles, so that while they slander you as wrongdoers, by observing your fine deeds they may glorify God on the day of inspection (I Pet. 2:11-12).

The theme of the **behavior** of the **resident alien** in a foreign land (alluded to in the introduction) now becomes dominant. Christians are in a community that practices much they must reject and fails to follow many things they must do. This community life, therefore, is often hostile to Christian living. The Christian will be different, and (as a result) will be mocked (or hated); often slanderous lies will be spread abroad about him. He must respond to these with a life style that refutes such lies and that honors God by attracting some to faith in Christ.

Peter has just spoken of this evangelistic purpose for which God called the believer into His kingdom (vs. 9): by both his **behavior** and his words, he is summoned to **declare God's virtues** to others. If God has such virtues, they ought to show in the lives of His children.

In a sense, much of what follows in this letter is an unfolding of verses 11, 12. The evangelistic task is given in more detail and applied specifically to particular circumstances and phases of life. These two verses form a general introduction to the more specific passages that follow. In what comes later on Peter explains how Christians may face up to and handle various types of persecution (e.g., by unsaved spouses, by tyrannical governments, etc.). But here, he simply says that in those places where God has placed them, believers must witness for Him by their **behavior.**

The **resident alien** was a person not so much on the move as one who had settled (at least temporarily) in a community. Often such **aliens** were licensed as such, and paid a small tax for the privilege of living in a foreign country. They were registered and recognized as **aliens.** That meant that they were *officially* **aliens,** and as such always on the spot.

Peter's readers were Jewish Christians who *literally* were **resident aliens** in Asia Minor, scattered by Jewish persecution when they became Christians (cf. comments on 1:1). In this second chapter Peters speaks of their **alien** status in two ways (both literally and figuratively). Surely, because of the dispersion (vs. 1) they understood the allusion and could appreciate the many nuances behind Peter's characterization of Christians as **resident aliens** in Satan's world-system.

As resident aliens and refugees, Peter urges them **to keep at a safe distance from fleshly desires.** There would be much in Satan's country to evoke such desires. But especially note the point that their status **as . . . aliens** required them to "hold back" (or **"distance themselves"**) from **fleshly desires.** Of course, *as Christians* they should do so, but the fact that Christians also are **aliens** in this world-system provides a powerful additional reason: they represent their heavenly empire, and (indeed) God Himself. It is not primarily for their own welfare or safety that they are to maintain exceptional behavior, although it is true that an **alien** always is in a vulnerable position. His rights are few and the protection that he receives from the state in which he resides may be minimal. But Peter is appealing to a higher motive that he reveals in verse 12: do so for God's honor and to win your Gentile neighbors to Christ. But we shall come to that presently.

Notice, now, that there is always an impending danger; it isn't easy to be the sorts of persons we ought to be. But the basic threat comes not from the *outside;* it comes from *within.* The world's temptations would cause no problem were it not for our own sinful desires. In the

Christian's own life is a mighty army, camped at the edge of the battlefield ready to march forth, challenge and often defeat his commitments and good intentions at a moment's notice. Peter makes this perfectly clear by his powerful figure of speech (**poised against your soul like an expeditionary force**) and urges **keep at a safe distance from** these **desires.** Failure to heed this admonition will lead to personal defeat and hishonor to the Name that he bears.

What is this mighty **expeditionary force?** It is none other than his own **fleshly desires** (note not *all* desires[16] but those that grow out of the **flesh).** What Peter means by the **flesh** is what Paul means in his frequent use of the term to describe the body, wrongly habituated to do (and has a **desire** to do) sinful things (for more on this problem and its solution, see my *Lectures on Counseling,* pp. 231-238). These **desires** are not necessarily gross **desires,** but any wrongly habituated responses that the body *wants* to make.[17]

Notice, once more, the basic solution given here is to **distance** one's self from the **desires** that are encamped over against his life **(soul).** They are ready to take him captive again even though he has been set free from the evil one. It is easy to give in to feeling and desire; it takes no effort to do so. All one need do is drift with his inclinations, taking the course of least resistance. But though this is easy, it is not the necessary course to follow; one doesn't have to be motivated in his decisions and actions by desire. He can change these patterns by exchanging them for biblical ones. The only person who can really overcome desire is the one who has an alternative response with which to replace it. This God has supplied in the commands of Scripture. The answer to desire-motivated living is commandment-motivated living.

First, one must become *aware* of the danger (this passage was de-

---

16. Christians are not opposed to desire or feeling, but rather are opposed to *fleshly* desire (which is so much a part of us still) and (as a result) to living a desire/feeling-oriented life (see comments on I Pet. 1:13, 14).

17. The body *wants* (desires) to make these sinful responses because it is habituated to do so. Habits are unconscious, comfortable, automatic responses. They develop from the sinful nature with which we are born. All sin, but each develops his own style of sinning that becomes habitual.

signed to bring about such awareness). He must also be aware of the biblical resources and method for averting the danger. If he knows *what* to do to avoid the danger (here, the key point is to **distance** himself from sinful desires, keeping out of range as earnestly as one would to avoid a hostile **army**), and if he prayerfully follows this biblical knowledge, he can succeed. Then, his life will honor God rather than bring disgrace on His Name.

"But," you ask, *"how* does one distance himself from his own **desires?"** By searching out those biblical commands that lead to alternative (God-pleasing) responses, by hiding these in his heart (cf. Ps. 119:11), and (at that time when **desire** grows strong and threatens to dominate his life) by interposing the biblical command between the **desire** and the decision. The only way to change from desire-oriented living is to develop (by study, preplanning and practice) Bible-oriented responses. It is impossible to run away from desire (there is no way to outdistance the army within, simply *because* it is within), so the only possible course of action feasible is to interpose the Word of God as a buffer between desires and decisions. Scripture alone can separate the two.

Peter's concern is not only for **good (fine) behavior,** but **fine behavior** *among the Gentiles* (unsaved) that (in spite of **slanderous** accusations) would (through **observation**) prove the falsity of these accusations to some of them who would **glorify God** on that great judgment **Day** when He comes to **inspect** and discover who has believed in Christ and who has not. Peter wants to see many **Gentile** converts **glorify God** as a consequence of the testimony that his readers' lives bore to them (cf. Matt. 5:15, 16).

This emphasis on **observed behavior** stresses the fact that Christians are watched. The emphasis will reappear in I Peter (cf. 3:1, 2), where he will declare that this is *the factor* that God honors in winning unsaved husbands/wives to Christ.

In those early days of the church, Christians were greatly **slandered;** even to the point of being accused of cannibalism.[18] People will be

---

18. Probably growing out of a misunderstanding of the Lord's Supper.

less inclined to believe **slander** when, with their own eyes, they experience the truth of Christianity in a Christian's life. Many who would never go to a Christian meeting to hear the gospel proclaimed, through **observation** would be able to see the effects of those truths upon human lives.

Instead of following human **desires** stemming from the **flesh,** a Christian who lives according to God's commands will be characterized by **fine deeds. Fine deeds** are good **deeds,** performed well (with finesse[19]). God asks not merely for conformity (of a perfunctory sort) but for enthusiastic, well-executed **obedience** (cf. 3:13). He cares about *how* we do what we do; not simply *that* we do it. And this is of special concern when living in the presence of unbelievers (cf. Col. 4:4, 6). In your sermon, illustrations of the shoddy way that people do much of the Lord's work are in order. In contrast, III John 6 offers a powerful comparison.

How may the two verses be preached? By combining ideas found in it as they revolve around the Holy Spirit's exhortation to **have good behavior among the Gentiles.**

Introduction: How well do you behave? At work? In social relations? None of my business? Your concern only? No! God has made it His concern; so it *is* my business. He cares about His Name and the unsaved persons around you. Indeed, He says . . .

I. YOU MUST BEHAVE WELL BEFORE UNBELIEVERS.
   A. You are a resident alien
   B. Whose life is under observation, and
   C. Who represents God before unbelievers
   D. By your words and deeds.
   E. God commands a life that will honor Him
   F. By attracting unbelievers to Christ.
II. YOUR DEEDS MUST HAVE FINESSE.

---

19. Well thought through, carefully planned, properly timed, etc. See my *Matters of Concern,* pp. 24-27, and *How to Overcome Evil,* pp. 70-74.

A. They must be not only good (i.e., conform to God's standards) but
B. They also must be fine (i.e., done with finesse),
C. Because God cares about *what* you do
D. And *how* you do it.
III. YOU MUST WIN THE WAR WITH DESIRE
A. To behave well.
B. Desires come from sinful response patterns
C. That are automatic, comfortable and unconscious.
D. These are like a powerful army poised against you
E. From which you must distance yourself
F. By interposing alternative scriptural responses.

Conclusion: Think of one or two areas (suggest a couple) in which you could improve. And get to work *this week,* beginning *today!*

Section Thirteen

Be submissive to every human authority for the Lord's sake, whether to the emperor, who is supreme, or to governors who are sent by him to take vengeance on evildoers and to praise those who do right. This is God's will: that by doing good you may muzzle the ignorant talk of foolish persons. As free persons, and not as those who use freedom as a cover-up for evil, live rather as God's slaves. Honor all men, love the brotherhood, fear God and honor the emperor (I Pet. 2:13-17).

Peter has set forth the general proposition that Christians must live before unbelievers in an exemplary way to dispel **slander**, to honor God's Name and to win unsaved persons to Christ (see comments on vss. 11, 12). Now he begins to specify. Since **governmental** agencies were (or would be) one prime source of persecution, Peter immediately turns to a discussion of Christian **behavior** toward the **government**. How do **resident aliens** (literally and figuratively) live under a **government** that is often hostile? The answer given is broad enough to apply to the relationship of Christians to rulers in general.

Submission forms the motif of the reply. In verses 13, 14 Peter enjoins **submission** to **all authorities,** including **the emperor,** who is the highest **authority,** and all those lesser ones who are under him. *All* governmental authority, at every level, must be respected as coming from God. The uniform Christian stance (cf. Rom. 13) was to recognize any valid government, paying taxes and obeying its laws. Revolution was never enjoined even in times of persecution or other gross perversions of power. (But I shall say more on this later.) It is not Christian to advocate the overthrow of a government in order to set it straight. Christians are opposed to anarchy because they recognize God as a God of law and order.

This stance is rooted in the truth that all valid governmental **authority** comes from God (Rom. 13:1). Governmental **authority** did not originate in a social compact, it does not derive from the consent of the governed or from the power of some to make their will dominant over others. **Government** is God-given. Christians, therefore, recognize government as a necessary factor in human society and show **respect** (vs. 17) for rulers.

Submission, then, is not conditioned upon the holiness or justice of the ruler. Rather, it is a matter of recognizing rightful **authority** as God's own **authority.** Christians may (as Christ did) call a ruler a "fox" (Luke 13:32), but may not resist his rightfully instituted **authority.** These words were an accurate description of Herod *as a man;* they had nothing to do with lack of submission. Christ also said, "Pay to Caesar what is his" (Luke 20:25; Rom. 13:5-7). So the Bible distinguishes the ruler *as a person* from the man *as a ruler.* It is in the latter capacity that he is to be respected and obeyed (the two elements of submission). Respect and obedience are called for because a ruler has authority conferred upon him by God. To respect this authority is to respect God Himself; to disobey, likewise, is to disregard God. That is what Peter means when he appends as a ground, **for the Lord's sake** (lit., "because of the Lord"). The **Lord** is Christ. Submission does not recognize an official as anything in and of himself; it is proper to submit because officially he represents God as a proponent of law and order in the world. Rule is God's prerogative; there is no power or **authority** elsewhere. Apart from Him, all assumed power is but a sham and a farce (Rom. 13:1, 2; John 19:10, 11). So, Christians **submit** to rulers because in exercising God's authority rulers serve Him (Rom. 13:4, 6).

Typically, rulers have not recognized the source of their **authority.** God has often brought them to their knees in order to make them do so (that is one dominant theme in the book of Daniel). Yet, in spite of this, Christian citizens **(resident aliens)** must **respect** the legitimate authority that they possess, as Daniel did. This is true even in the face of persecution.

But **submission** to rulers isn't absolute because the authority God gave them isn't unlimited. It is circumscribed by Scripture. The apostles **submitted** to legitimate **authority** exercised by rulers, but when rulers went *beyond* that **authority,** they no longer spoke with **authority;** instead they spoke with human **authority.** This was recognized by the apostles, who disobeyed and justified their disobedience in these words: "We must obey God rather than men" (cf. Acts 5:28, 29; 4:19, 20).

God's **authority** invested in each sphere (the state, the home, the church, business) never conflicts with His **authority** in another. The **authority** of each is defined and delimited in the Bible. Civil disobedience may occur only when rulers, acting on purely human **authority,** *require* Christians to sin.

Of what does governmental **authority**[20] consist and what are its bounds? Largely this authority is comprehended in the statement that lesser rulers **are sent by him** (the ruler) or **by Him** (God)[21] **to take vengeance on wrongdoers and to praise those who do right** (vs. 14). To maintain law and order by the exercise of force, and to levy taxes to support such activities, are the legitimate functions of governments (cf. Rom. 13).

Typically governments exceed their God-given **authority** to reach into areas of social service, education, health, etc. (that ought to be exercised by the home or the church). This tendency has been a cause of much harmful legislation and difficulty for Christians. Rulers are required to *punish* and to *praise,* but the Bible says nothing of an obligation to *provide.*

Governmental **authority** also is limited to regulating **behavior;** i.e., *outward* actions. Peter speaks of rulers responding to those who *do* **evil** or **good.** Rulers have no right to bind the conscience. Both lesser and **supreme** rulers (duly constituted as such) must be respected and obeyed.

In verse 15, a second reason for submission is appended: God

---

20. The word *authority* (vs. 13), literally, is created or "instituted" authority. There is no obligation to submit to improperly instituted or self-assumed authority.
21. Either way, God ultimately does so.

wants (**this is God's will**) to **muzzle the ignorant talk of foolish persons.** Christians were accused of being radicals, troublemakers and revolutionaries. Because they refused to submit to Caesar *as a divine being,* they were thought to be subversive. But this was due to **ignorance** of God and Christian belief. **Foolish persons** (a fool is one who speaks *beyond* his knowledge and/or against the facts) misunderstood and spread falsehood everywhere. **Submission** to rulers would counter such **foolish** talk. Note in the Greek the alliteration (using four words beginning with alpha) used in this sentence; Peter had voiced the idea before and had a well-framed response to the problem. The **slander** is **slander** *because* it comes from wilful **ignorance,** originating in a rejection of Christ.

Verse 16 presents an interesting insight into the Christian's status. The Christian is not a subject of any earthly kingdom, and in reality he is exempt from (**free** from) its laws and regulations. He is a citizen of the empire from the heavens. He is **free** from all human **authority** and all human institutions. Peter's words echo Christ's in Matthew 17:24-27, where **free** = exempt (cf. vs. 26). Christians don't really take orders from human beings; they submit to Christ. Why then obey rulers? Peter brings up this question of **freedom** only to anticipate a specious argument that might be made in order to cut it down before it sprouts leaves. Some might say, "If **free,** we don't have to **submit** to government." Peter replies, "Wrong! Christians have not been set **free** from *all* **authority;** the **freedom** that they have actually makes them God's slaves (cf. Rom. 6:22). **Freedom** doesn't mean anarchy. It is **freedom** to do good. As God's slaves, they must obey Him. And we see that He Himself has commanded **submission** to rulers. Therefore, we **submit** to rulers because we want to **submit** to God.

Thus, Christian **freedom** never may be used as **a cloak to cover up evil** (disobedience to God). On this tendency, cf. Jude 4. It is interesting that such persons (as Jude observes) are those who follow their own desires rather than God's commandments (cf. Jude 16, 18; contrast I Peter 2:11, etc.). What our freedom means is that we serve God, not men. Christian counselors (and others) should be alert to the possibility of such a cover up among those who very strongly advocate freedom.

Finally, Peter puts it all into perspective—Christians must **honor all men** (i.e., show proper regard wherever it is due), but especially must show **love** to the brotherhood (cf. Gal. 6:10). Also, they must **fear** (show awe and respect for) God, and if they do so, they will **honor the emperor.**

Let's now gather these verses together:

Introduction: Are you upset with the government? Disapprove of state or national policies? As a Christian, what should be your stance toward politicians and their policies?

    I. YOU MUST SUBMIT TO GOVERNMENTAL AUTHORITIES
       A. Because God commands it.
       B. Submission means obedience and respect
       C. To rulers clothed with God's authority,
       D. Including both supreme and lesser authorities.
   II. YOU MUST SUBMIT TO EVERY VALID LAW
       A. God gave rulers authority
       B. To punish wrongdoers,
       C. To praise those who do right,
       D. And to levy taxes
       E. In order to promote law and order.
  III. YOU MUST NOT SUBMIT TO INVALID LAWS
       A. Made by rulers who exceed the limits of their authority
       B. And, on occasion, require Christians to sin.
       C. In those cases, Christians must obey God rather than men.
  IV. YOU MUST DO THIS
       A. As freed persons who don't use freedom as a cover for sin
       B. But honor God, by serving Him
       C. In order to muzzle ignorant slanderers
       D. And to show respect to all rightful authority (vs. 17).

Conclusion: What practices in your political life need to be changed?

Section Fourteen

Household servants, submit yourselves to your masters, showing full respect, not only to those who are good and lenient but also to those who are cruel. One finds favor if, out of conscience toward God, he bears up under pain when suffering unjustly. Indeed, what credit is coming to you if when you are beaten for sinning you endure it? But if you endure suffering for doing good, this finds favor with God. In fact, you were called to this, since Christ Himself suffered in your place, leaving behind a pattern for you to copy so that you might follow in His steps: "He committed no sin, nor was deceit found in His mouth." When He was insulted, He returned no insults; when He suffered, He made no threats, but entrusted Himself to the One Who does judge righteously. He Himself bore our sins in His body on the tree, so that by dying to sins we might live to righteousness ("By His wounds you were healed"). You were wandering like sheep, but now you have turned back to the Shepherd and Overseer of your souls (I Pet. 2:18-25).

Submission under trial and persecution is the theme that runs throughout this section. First, Peter considered **submission** to governmental authority (vss. 13-17). In chapter 3 he will urge the **submission** of wives to unsaved husbands. Here, the emphasis falls upon **submission** in work. Specifically, **slaves** and **masters** are in view. During this discussion, Peter takes the opportunity to set forth the greatest of all examples of **submission**—Christ's **submission** during unjust treatment (vss. 21-25).

Household servants[22] are addressed in verse 18. These domestics

---

22. The same word is used in Luke 16:13, "No household servant can be a slave to two masters."

probably are singled out as an example of one of the most demeaning and difficult of all working relationships. But though **slaves** are mentioned, what Peter says contains principles of *abiding value for* every working relationship (cf. also Col. 3:22-25; Eph. 6:5-7; I Tim. 6:1f.; Tit. 2:9f.). On slavery in general, see John T. Demarest's comments on this verse in his commentary on I Peter.

The **master** mentioned here is called a *despot,* a term that decribed an absolute owner. Despots, in Roman law, possessed even the power of life and death over their slaves.

Full respect must be shown to despots, whether they are **kind** or **cruel** (lit., "crooked"). **Respect,** again, does not depend on anything in the **master** himself. Equal **respect** must be **shown** to both sorts of **masters.** It makes no difference what he is like since the Christian must **show respect out of a conscience toward God.** That is to say, there is an internal motive. He doesn't **show respect** in order to receive (or because he has received) good treatment from his **master;** his concern is **God's** response. He wants to please Him. Thus

1. no slave could excuse his bad behavior on the basis of bad treatment by his master;
2. a slave could work in joy, satisfaction and with enthusiasm because he was working for God (cf. Col. 3; Eph. 6).

If, during **unjust suffering** and **grief** (pain) the **slave bears up** well (i.e., doesn't threaten, curse, etc.), takes it and prays for his **master,** God takes notice of this, and the **slave finds favor** in *His* sight. He will not forget; He will commend ("well done . . .") and will reward (cf. Col. 3). God will avenge the injustice done and bless the slave (cf. Rom. 12:14ff.). But if he **suffers for** his own **sin,** and takes a **beating** well, there is **no credit** for this. Counselors will find this verse a powerful antidote to the problem of persons who wallow in self-pity. People may commiserate with them, but God doesn't. He shows His favor toward and blesses those who **endure suffering for doing good.** Note:

(1) God doesn't bless those who are merely passive sufferers. It is those who **do good** while suffering to whom he shows **favor.**

(2) Here Peter once again returns to his major emphasis—doing **good** in **suffering.**

The tendency when suffering unjustly is to retaliate or to sit and sulk. Neither response is Christian; both focus upon self rather than upon God and one's neighbor. The biblical response is the response of love: how can I honor God and bless those who are persecuting me? This alternative calls for **doing good,** praying, etc. It demands an outward look rather than an inward one. And as a by-product (it can never be the goal or purpose of the action) one suffers less. It is certain that the person who focuses upon his own suffering, misfortune and pain thereby intensifies it. The Christian must respond by *doing good* (Rom. 12:21), the most powerful way to overcome evil.[23] The key is to *continue* to **do good.** God has not treated him unjustly; therefore, he should continue to **do good** to serve and honor God, for Whom he really works as a slave.

Peter makes it clear that **unjust suffering** should be a surprise to no one. When God **called** them, it was made clear that this was in the offing (cf. 3:9; II Thess. 3:3). Why should the disciple expect better treatment than his Master? Indeed, Christ set for us **a pattern to copy,** demonstrating Himself how to **endure** suffering. The word translated **pattern to copy** refers to a sample of handwriting given to children to use as a model when learning how to write. They would trace over it and **copy** it out. Christians, Peter says, are to use Christ's example as a **pattern** for their own responses when facing undeserved trials. Step by step, they are to **follow in His steps** (footprints, tracks). What follows is a partial description of some of that pattern, isolating some of the elements that make it up.

(1) He **committed no sin** (cf. Isa. 53:9; Zeph. 3:13). Sin cannot be excused by saying that suffering brings about extenuating circumstances. Christ faced suffering more profound than all others, yet He didn't sin. We, too, are to remember that there is no excuse for sin—even in situations that involve extreme pain.

---

23. On this see my book on Romans 12:14-21, entitled *How to Overcome Evil.*

(2) **Nor was deceit found in His mouth.** Even if one searched for it (that is the thrust of the verb **found**), **deceit** could not be located in Him. **Deceit** was a problem frequently encountered among slaves, for which they often suffered justly.

(3) **He . . . entrusted Himself to the One who does judge justly.** Others—masters on earth—may not, but God *always* judges justly. He **entrusted** (lit., "handed over") His life to the Father, believing that He would do the right thing in trial. There is a contrast between God and others who do not act justly (cf. 4:19).

Peter mentions other facts about Christ's death that are not a part of the **Pattern,** and we need not (indeed, we *cannot* **copy** them because they are a part of His redemptive sacrifice for sins:

(1) **He Himself** (an intensive pronoun is used: *He* did it; not some other) **bore our sins in His own body on the tree** (Isa. 53:12; Deut. 21:23). As our substitute He bore the burden of guilt and punishment that we deserved to carry for our sins.

(2) **By His wounds you are healed** (Isa. 53:3, 5). This, remember, was written to slaves, many of whom had felt the lash on their own backs.

(3) This vicarious, penal, substitutionary sacrifice brought about the following results:

(a) Those who have believed in Him are **healed** (forgiven) of their sins;

(b) They are now able **to live new lives of righteousness,** freed from the power of sin.

(c) **Straying sheep** (Isa. 53:6) without protection or guidance have now **returned** to the Shepherd and Overseer Who sought and found the hundredth sheep.

Introduction: Did you ever complain, "My boss treats me like a slave"? Well, let's see how God says slaves should act.

I. YOU MUST SUBMIT TO YOUR MASTER.
   A. Submission means obedience and respect
   B. Regardless of how he treats you
   C. Because you really serve God out of conscience.
   D. He doesn't mistreat you,
   E. And He looks upon you with favor
   F. If you bear up under unjust suffering
   G. And do good.
II. YOU SHOULDN'T BE SURPRISED AT SUFFERING UNJUSTLY
   A. You were aware of it at your calling, and
   B. Christ suffered unjustly;
   C. The disciple isn't above his Master.
III. HE HAS LEFT YOU A PATTERN FOR ENDURANCE
   A. Christ's own example—
   B. He never sinned
   C. Never spoke deceitfully
   D. Though He suffered more than all.
   E. He never returned evil for evil
   F. But put His life in God's hands
   G. Because He would treat Him justly.
IV. BUT THERE ARE THINGS HE DID THAT YOU CAN'T DO
   A. He died vicariously for your sins
   B. Brought "healing" from sin
   C. Made possible a new life of righteousness
   D. And became your Shepherd and Overseer
   E. To protect and guide you in times of trial
   F. So that you won't have to face it alone (Phil. 2:13).

Conclusion: Behave submissively toward your superiors at work, and continue to do good even if you are treated unfairly. You really serve Christ, Who cares for you and rewards your faithfulness.

CHAPTER THREE

Section Fifteen

In the same way, wives, submit yourselves to your own husbands, so that even if some of them disobey the Word they may be won without a word through the behavior of their wives, by observing your respectful, pure behavior. Your adornment must consist not of outward things such as the braiding of hair, and putting on of gold jewelry or clothing yourselves with robes; rather, beautify the hidden person of your heart with the incorruptible quality of a gentle and quiet spirit, which is of great value before God. Indeed, in this way also holy women of the past who put their hope in God beautified themselves, submitting to their own husbands, as, for example, when Sarah obeyed Abraham, calling him lord. And you will have become her children by doing good and fearing no intimidation (I Pet. 3:1-6).

Chapter three is of special significance to persons married to an unsaved spouse.[1] The first six verses detail God's requirement for a Christian **wife** in such a situation, showing her how to live and relate to her **husband** in a manner that pleases God and that *may* (in time) **win** her husband to Christ. While no absolute assurance that he will be saved is given, the hope is held out as a distinct (and not remote) possibility. If God will use her to bring her husband to Jesus as his Savior, clearly this is how she will be used.

On the other hand, it must be made clear that God expects her to

---

1. Peter first sets up the problem in terms of a Christian wife/non-Christian husband because he has been discussing successively various submission contexts in which the Christian often suffers because he is in submission to an unsaved authority. He briefly mentions the reverse situation (note **likewise** in verse 7) next.

conform to the prescriptions that He gives here whether her husband comes to faith in Christ or not. She cannot follow Peter's directions and make changes in an outward, superficial manner as a gimmick to **win** her spouse. Indeed, Peter calls for a radical **inner** change of the **heart** (the **inner** life one lives before God and himself) that **beautifies** the **inner** life and, consequently, leads to **gentle, quiet** and **submissive** outward **behavior.** Her concern must be to become the sort of wife that God requires, whether her husband becomes a Christian or not— *just to please God!*[2] Now let us turn to God's requirements and directions.

First, God specifically forbids preaching at her **husband (without a word)** or nagging him with the gospel if he **disobeys the Word** (cf. 1:22; 2:8; 3:20, where obedience/disobedience to the **Word** means trusting/rejecting the Good News. See especially comments on 1:22). The point to get across is that the Christian **wife** should not expect to **win** her **husband** by verbal means (witnessing to him, turning on Christian radio broadcasts for him to listen to, leaving tracts all over the house, etc.). Instead, God orders her to stop all that and *demonstrate* her faith! Consequently, in counseling, it may be profitable to say to a **wife** something like this:

"You may preach at him day and night, but you'll only drive him further from the gospel. Your words are like bullets bouncing off a tank! There is only one way to penetrate his defenses: a genuine, demonstrable and lasting change in you—in your actions and in your attitudes. And it must begin with an inward change of heart. When, every day, you are becoming more and more what God wants you to be and more and more doing what God wants you to do, then things will begin to happen. You will be happier and your husband will be affected; you will begin to find your way through the chinks in his armor. If this week you are the best wife in the neighborhood, by next week you become the best in town and (if you keep on this way much

---

2. Very often, before going further, a counselor must debate the counselee's agenda with him till in repentance he replaces the humanistic, man-centered elements with godly, Christ-centered ones.

longer) you will soon become the best wife in the state, you will get through to him. Husbands are impervious to your preaching; but a man can take only so much of a wife who is plainly improving at a rapid pace, and shows no signs of stopping. This sort of change, I assure you, will soon shatter the status quo! Both you and your husband will change. If you change, he must respond differently. Some husbands say, 'Tell me more about your change'; others may say, 'I didn't bargain for a wife like this,' and leave home (in counseling, we see *both* responses). But either way, the status quo also will change."

Notice, Peter doesn't allow the wife to say, "If I had a Christian husband, *then* I could live as a Christian wife should." No! No excuses are recognized. In a context that presupposes suffering (**in the same way** refers back to Christ's sufferings described at the end of chapter 2; note also the word about **fearing no intimidation,** vs. 6), the emphasis falls solely upon the wife's responsibility. Living as a Christian *does not depend upon anyone else*. If her husband *never* comes to Christ (or if he trusts Christ at her funeral), she can live a fruitful, righteous, satisfying life. The point of the passage is that when she does, God may use this to point her husband to the gospel; it is not the other way around! Yet many women continually complain, "I could be different if only. . . ." Forget the "If onlys . . ." and the "If . . . thens," God says. It is possible to live an exemplary Christian life with an unsaved spouse—who persecutes you! This is a vital point to make. A key factor in counseling is to sort out responsibilities.[3] Bad **behavior** cannot be blamed on someone else.

When a husband **disobeys the Word** (pays no attention to the gospel), he may be reached **by observing** the gospel at work in his **wife's respectful behavior** (vs. 2). Peter doesn't mean to say that anyone could be saved apart from a knowledge of the good news (Christ's death and resurrection for sinners), but pictures a situation in which he presupposes that the husband has already heard the

---

3. For more on this see my book, *Matters of Concern*, pp. 20-23.

message (from his wife, if not from others) and had rejected (**disobeyed**) it. Her **behavior** can reawaken an interest in it.

If her **behavior** is important, then she must know what sort of **behavior wins.** Peter's emphasis basically falls upon **submission** (cf. Eph. 5:22-24, 33; and for more on both passages, see my book *Christian Living in the Home*).

What is **submission?** In this passage (and in Eph. 5) two elements appear:

(1) **obedience** (vs. 6).

(2) **respect** (vs. 2).

These two elements are the basic components of **submission. Obedience** speaks of *action;* **respect** of *attitude.* The former has to do with *what* she does; the latter with *how* she does it. Both are important; indeed, the absence of one will cancel out the effect of the other.

Respect (vs. 2) is the manner in which **obedience** must be carried out. It is counterproductive to **obey** in a **disrespectful** way. The value of the **obedience** is destroyed by the temptation to become hostile that disrespect places in the way.

"But how can I **respect** a man like my husband?" many women ask. The answer is similar to the one given earlier when discussing **respect** for rulers (cf. comments on 2:13-17). A Christians must respect the uniform with which God clothed husbands, even if they poorly fit it. The **respect** is directed toward God and His authority, not fundaméntally toward the man in whom it is invested. When a wife speaks disrespectfully toward her husband, she really speaks in a manner that disregards *God.* That is serious.

Obedience is the second element (cf. vs. 6). A Christian wife must do everything her husband requires—short of sinning. God never gave a husband (or anyone else) the authority to require another to sin. Whenever a person does so, he does it *on his own authority alone!*

In verses 3, 4 Peter contrasts **inner** and **outer** beauty. One is artificial; it is added to the person. The other is genuine because it is the result of a change in the person herself. **Adornment** must be **inward; the inner person of the heart** must become **beautiful** in order to please

God and to be **winning.** This **hidden person,** when so transformed, will become visible.

Women who try to hold **husbands** or **win husbands** only by making themselves **outwardly** attractive misunderstand the fact that **husbands** really want a woman who is *herself* attractive **within.** **Respect** and **obedience** that issue in lasting values (of **incorruptible quality** in contrast to **outer** corruptible **adornments**), such as **a gentleness and quietness** are *most* alluring and winsome. Wives who carp and criticize, who whine and whinny, who yell and scream, who argue and act stubbornly fail to exhibit this **inner beauty.** **The gentle and quiet spirit** (spirit here means *attitude* and *approach*) attracts; other attitudes and approaches repel.

Peter observes that this has always been the case (vs. 5) with women who believed in **God,** who 'fixed' their expectations (**hope**) on Him (cf. comments on **hope** in 1:3). Then (vs. 6), he cites a specific example of a **submissive** wife in which both elements (**respect, obedience**) are discernible. **Sarah obeyed** Abraham and called him lord (**respect** that acknowledged his position as head of the home).

It is important to note the qualification that follows those words in verse 6: **wives** today become **Sarah's children** (i.e., will be like her, and called **submissive**) by

(1) **doing good** and
(2) **fearing no intimidation.**

This observation is important because some have misapplied verse 6a by referring it to sinful acts, thus making Sarah an example of **obedience** in committing sin. Nothing could be further from Peter's mind! Clearly, in the context, one becomes **her child** *only by doing good.* There would be no reason to **fear intimidation** (and no reason to warn against doing so) if the wife did not draw the line at sinning. All legitimate requests are to be **obeyed.** Otherwise a wife must endure unjust suffering and continue to **do good** regardless of consequences. **Doing good** rarely leads to more suffering (cf. vss. 13, 14), but regardless, she is to be a zealot for **doing good.** And **doing good** is God's way of overcoming evil (vss. 8, 9; cf. Rom. 12:14-21). She still respects the husband's uniform even if she must reject his enticement to sin. She says "no," **respectfully!**

The crucial fact to point out in preaching and counseling is that no wife need sit, suffer and sulk! **Submission** is not passive but active! She seeks to **win** her **husband** to Christ. The word **win** (vs. 1) is a military term. She is to declare war on her husband and attempt to take him captive for Christ. But the weapons she uses are to be **obedience, respect, gentleness and quietness,** and her basic strategy is to overcome his evil by **doing good** (see my book, *How to Overcome Evil*). Such **submission** is not doormatism. It is aggressive, violent **submission** bent on defeating evil by **doing good!** No Christian wife need sit still, having nothing to do about the situation; God has given battle orders. To sit in self-pity is sin!

Counselors and preachers have much to communicate. The concepts recorded here have been either distorted or ignored by many. For further counseling observations growing out of this passage, see my *Matters of Concern for Christian Counselors*, pp. 85, 86. Now, put it together:

Introduction: How do you live with an unbelieving husband? I didn't ask how do you *win* him, even though that also is involved, because the basic question is, "How do you live to please Christ?," whether you are able to lead your husband to Him or not.

   I. YOU MUST EVANGELIZE HIM
       A. Not by preaching at him
       B. But by *demonstrating* the power of the gospel
       C. In your behavior.
  II. YOU MUST SUBMIT TO YOUR HUSBAND
       A. Even if he is unsaved
       B. By respecting him
       C. For the authority that he bears
       D. And by obeying him
       E. In every request that isn't sinful.

III. YOU MUST CHANGE
A. Not only outwardly,
B. As a gimmick to win your husband.
C. But there must be an inward change
D. Leading to inner (rather than outer) beauty
E. That issues in gentleness and quietness
F. And good deeds
G. In spite of intimidation.

Conclusion: Start today. If you don't know how to begin, one way is to make a list of all the ways that you are failing God as a woman, a wife and a mother. Then, start doing what God says to do about each. Do good, regardless of intimidation.

Section Sixteen

Husbands, likewise live with your wives in an under-standing way, showing respect for the woman as you would a fragile vase, and as joint heirs of the grace of life, so that your prayers may not be interrupted (I Pet. 3:7).

What about **husbands?** Lest that question be asked and no response found, Peter anticipates and succinctly—but powerfully—answers it. I shall deal with this verse only in brief in the most fundamental way, since I have a taped sermon on it available.[4]

Husbands are addressed directly, and commanded (whether their **wives** are saved or unsaved; Peter makes no distinction) to be careful and considerate about how they **live** with them. They must stop living in ignorance of their **wives'** problems, desires, needs, longings, fears, etc. (as so many man do who have never bothered to try to come to an **understanding** of them), but, literally, "according to knowledge" = **in an understanding way.**

The old cliché, "You'll never **understand** a woman," must be squelched. **Husbands** need to be told—as, indeed, Peter tells them— "There is *one* woman you must **understand:** *your* woman! God commands it!"

"But how does one **undestand a woman?**" many men will reply. In the tape (see footnote 4 for details) I have answered this question in depth for any who wish to explore it further. Fundamentally, here, I may simply suggest that a husband will **understand a woman** only

---

4. For the tape, write to Christian Study Services, 1790 East Willow Grove Ave., Laverock, PA 19118.

if he makes a careful study of her through the loving giving of one's self in which he takes the time to do so.

The **respect** that a husband must show to a **wife** is based upon the fact that she is a **woman** who, together with her husband, is a **(joint)- heir** of the **grace** (unmerited gift) of eternal **life** (cf. 1:10 for this use of grace). This means that

(1) She is not inferior to her husband as a person

(2) She will receive equal reward and status with her husband at Christ's coming.

This **respect,** then, should grow out of the loving concern that God has shown toward the woman. And it should be evidenced by the way that her husband treats her—he should treat her as he would a weaker vessel (or **fragile container**). Many men treat their wives as they would an old tin garbage can. "Not so," says Peter; "you must treat her as you would treat **a fragile vase,** Ming dynasty!" This call for gentleness parallels Paul's exhortation to **nourish and cherish wives** *as* their own bodies (Eph. 5:28, 29).

If a husband refuses to live in this way, it will interfere with his prayers (**your** is plural and refers to the **husbands** addressed). Why should a **husband** expect God to honor his requests when he dishonors his **wife,** fails to treat her as a gentle man should, and makes no effort to **understand** her? God has bestowed upon her equal eternal honor; then why shouldn't he show her every consideration now?

I shall suggest no outline since that can be developed from the cassette tape on the subject (see footnote 4).

Section Seventeen

Finally, all of you, be of one mind, compassionate, full of brotherly love, tenderhearted, humbleminded, not returning evil for evil or insult for insult, but on the contrary, blessing others, since you were called to do this so that you may inherit a blessing: "He who would love life and see good days must keep his tongue from evil and his lips from speaking deceitful words. Let him turn away from evil and let him do good. Let him seek peace and pursue it. The Lord's eyes are on the righteous and His ears are open to their prayer. But the Lord's face is against those who are doing evil (I Pet. 3:8-12).

When Peter says **finally,** he is not like many preachers who have trouble bringing their sermons in for a landing. They approach the runway with a **finally,** only to go zooming off into the blue again to take another spin around the field. Here the word **finally** is appropriate because it marks the conclusion of the section on **submission** that is in these verses coming to a close.

Peter sums up much of what he has been saying while supplementing these exhortations with a call to unity and mutual concern (vs. 8). Christians must treat one another this way in all cases; but the need is paramount in times of persecution. This unity and mutual concern caps off the witness of good behavior to the unsaved world. When Christians fight one another, they weaken their war against evil. An army, divided against itself, will lose. They must **be of one mind.**

Five exhortations comprise Peter's words to Christians (**all of you**) regarding their relationship to one another:

1. **Be of one mind.** This is the positive way of saying "don't

quarrel." Unity comes, as Philippians 2 demonstrates, when believers (like their Lord) put others first, and focus their concern on the welfare of others (vss. 1-3). That is why the four exhortations that follow all emphasize the loving giving of one's self to his brothers.

2. **Compassionate** (literally, sympathetic). The sympathy (or compassion), however, is not merely an attitude. Rather, it is an attitude that issues in acts. It denotes "sharing the experiences of another" (Moulton and Milligan). If a Christian never enters into another's circumstances, he will never appreciate or understand his brother's joys, problems, heartaches, etc. The **compassionate** Christian cannot help but "weep with those who weep and rejoice with those who rejoice."

3. **Full of brotherly love** (the word **full** is not in the original but is supplied to give the sense). For more on **brotherly love**, see comments on 1:22.

4. **Tenderhearted.** The word denotes a warm and tender attitude. It speaks of rich emotion. In the midst of trial and suffering it is easy to become self-centered, nursing one's own wounds. One can become callous without even recognizing it. The Christian may not do so; and he will not if he cultivates **tenderheartedness.** This is done by taking an interest in others and learning to be sensitive to their emotions.

5. **Humbleminded.** The humble person is not only one who refrains from boasting and bragging; positively, he also rejoices over the successes of others and puts them forward rather than himself. This is the "mind" (attitude) that was in Christ Jesus (Phil. 2).

In verse 9 the general biblical principle that has been expressed in this letter already, and that frequently occurs elsewhere (Rom. 12:17; I Thess. 5:15) is asserted. The Christian response to evil doing is doing good. Revenge is never allowed. That God should require this in suffering ought to come as no surprise to Christians; they were **called** to live this way. They were **called** to be a blessing (to bless others is to say and do good to them) and thus to **inherit a blessing.**

This is no new experiment; it was made clear to them at the outset

103

of their Christian life—from their **call** to become part of Christ's family and army. Too frequently today, no such explanation is given to new converts. Then, when trial and suffering come, they wonder why. And even when they get past that question, they don't know how to handle suffering. To teach about the trials of being a Christian should be a high priority item for Christian workers.

Peter says that if his readers are a **blessing** to others (even to those who persecute them), God will see to it that they too are **blessed.** The **blessing** that they **inherit** has been thought by some to refer to eternal life; by others to this life. From the passage quoted in verses 10-12 as support for this assertion (Ps. 34:13-17), it seems clear that Peter is speaking about **blessing** here and now.

God does not intend for His people to be a dour, unhappy lot. There was a strain of Puritanism that glorified this sort of thing. In the current revival of Puritanism, it is important to be alert to this sad and non-Christian emphasis. Right now, a Christian can know happiness and joy even in persecution and suffering (cf. 1:6-9). One of the major reasons why there is not more **blessedness** among Christians is because of the misery that they bring upon themselves by sin. Peter wants to avoid all unnecessary suffering of this sort.

When Christians fail to **return** (or pay back) **blessing** for **evil** and **insult,** they thereby forfeit some of the **blessings** of their present **inheritance.** These blessings come both automatically (since "it is more blessed to give than to receive") and by being conferred upon them by God. In both the way that God constituted human nature, and in His providential **blessings** given to those who follow His commands, the heir receives a part of his present **inheritance.**

The psalm quoted (Ps. 34:13-17) in verses 10-12 tells Christians that when they **do good** (i.e., live as God pleases and please God by their living), they **see** (i.e., come to know by experience) **good days,** the **Lord's eyes are on them** (i.e., He sees, recognizes and rewards such behavior), and He hears (answers) their **prayer.** In contrast, those Christians who **do evil** find only a grim frown on His **face.** When **the Lord's face is against them,** nothing that they do prospers (cf. vs. 7 about failure in **prayer**).

The exhortations that grow out of these facts are both negative and positive:

Negative:
1. **Keep** your **tongue from evil** and your **lips from speaking deceitful words;**
2. **Turn away from evil.**

Positive:
1. **Do good;**
2. **Seek peace and pursue it** (i.e., hunt it down like a hound; do all you can to find it; cf. Heb. 12:14; Rom. 12:18).

In summary, Peter says, don't start or bring about more trouble by your mouth (cf. chapter on "How to Manage Your Mouth," in *How to Overcome Evil*). Get away from all the temptation that you can, and (instead) plunge headlong into the quest for **peace** with everyone. Don't give up; *pursue* **peace**—track it down till you find it!

The Christian must not be a troublemaker; he is to be a peacemaker. The passages on **submission** are all directed toward achieving **peace** by every honorable means (i.e., in every biblically legitimate way possible). Thus, the quotation is a fitting conclusion to the questions Peter has been discussing. Here is one way to tie it all together:

Introduction: Are you living in peace and blessing? Do you foster it? Or do you constantly find yourself disturbed by unhappy interpersonal relations?

I. YOU CAN LIVE IN PEACE . . .
   A. If you seek unity with other Christians
   B. By compassionately entering into their experiences,
   C. By expressing brotherly love,
   D. By cultivating tenderness,
   E. By not allowing yourself to become callous
   F. And by remaining noble.
II. WHEN OTHERS WRONG YOU . . .

A. Don't pay back evil for evil; insult for insult
B. But bless those who wrong you,
C. Keeping your mouth from causing more trouble,
D. Fleeing all temptations to evil
E. And earnestly pursuing peace till you find it.
F. Then God will bless *you*.

Conclusion: Examine your life right now. Toward whom must you change some behavior? Decide *specifically* what God would have you do instead to seek peace—and do it!

Section Eighteen

And who will harm you if you become enthusiasts for good? Yet, even if you should suffer because of righteousness, you must be happy. In fact, you must not even fear their threat, nor be upset. Instead, in your hearts, sanctify Christ as Lord, always ready to defend the hope that is in you to everybody who asks you. But do so with gentleness and respect. Have a good conscience so that when you are slandered, those who speak insultingly about your good behavior in Christ may be put to shame. So you see, it is better to suffer for doing good, if God's plan has so determined, than to suffer for doing evil (I Pet. 3:13-17).

Ordinarily **good behavior** leads to peace and quiet. By **doing good** there is more likelihood of it; taking revenge (vs. 9) and stirring up trouble by inflammatory words (vs. 10) brings trial and suffering. Such is the general rule, and such is the import of Peter's rhetorical question in verse 13. The answer implied is "hardly anyone."

Christians, therefore, must become **enthusiasts** (lit. "zealots") **for good**. A zealot or **enthusiast** is someone who is bent on seeing something happen. Whatever that something is, he talks it, he walks it he eats it, he sleeps it (cf. sports **enthusiasts** of various sorts in preaching). And, because he is caught up in this, an **enthusiast** is known for his particular concerns. He is identified with them (and they with him). This is the connection that a Christian must have with **good**. Ask the listener, "By any stretch of the imagination, would anyone call you an **enthusiast for good?** If not, some changes need to be made."

There is an exception to the general rule stated in verse 13; Peter realistically and wisely notes the fact. While **good** often softens some, others grow hardened by it. This is true especially in those situations where the **goodness** of a Christian life stands in stark contrast to evil in the life of an unbeliever, exposing him for what he is. Then, he may "hate the light" that exposes his sin and try to extinguish it. In such cases, it is possible for a Christian to **suffer** unjustly **because of righteousness,** just as his Lord did (vs. 18). But an **enthusiast** for good will persist; adverse circumstances (here refer back to your sporting illustrations, etc.) will not deter him or cause him to slacken his interest or activities. He will go on regardless.

Nevertheless, he **must** still **be happy** in such circumstances (Matt. 5:10; Acts 5:41). How is that possible? The theme of joy in suffering is not new (see comments on 1:6-8). However, referring to Isaiah 8:11-13 does make a new and most significant point. He says it isn't right even **to fear their threat** or **be upset. To fear their threat** is (lit.) "to **fear** their fear." Isaiah seemed to speak about having the same fear as others. However, Peter takes him to mean to **fear** what the enemy attempts to make you **fear** (a **threat**). He goes so far as to insist that in time of danger the believer need not even be **upset.** Here, Peter may have been thinking of his own three denials of Christ out of **fear** (vs. 15 may also reflect concerns growing out of that experience).

This unwillingness to **fear threats** is a large order. Yet, whatever God requires of His children He provides. We can be sure that there are biblical directions for overcoming **fear** and there is power provided by the Holy Spirit to carry them out. What are these directions? They are found in verses 15, 16:

1. **Sanctify Christ as Lord in your hearts;**
2. **Always be ready to defend the hope that is in you to everybody who asks you;**
3. **With gentleness and respect;**
4. From **a good conscience**
5. That grows out of **good behavior.**

Whenever this fist full of factors is present, any Christian can face danger unruffled and unperturbed; he can put down **slanderous** accusations against himself and his Lord, and he can **put to shame those who speak insultingly** about him. It is important, therefore, to understand each of these factors and to be sure that our lives are characterized by them *at all times*. These factors are the outgrowth of love.[5]

To **sanctify** ("set apart," see comments on 1:2) here means to clearly identify by setting Him apart from all other allegiances. It is also to set Him apart from all questions or doubts. Perhaps, best expressed, it is to *plainly recognize* Christ as Lord. When a believer **sanctifies Christ *as Lord*** (the Jehovah of the O.T. Who now rules His church and every member of it, Who promises to care for him and to shepherd him throughout his life), he need not **fear** or **be upset.** Here are some of the implications of recognizing (**sanctifying**) **Christ as Lord:**

1. The believer is not alone; Christ knows all about the threat.
2. Christ cares for him and will do what is best in his life.
3. Circumstances are not out of control, nor are they meaningless.
4. Christ has a good purpose in all this.
5. Christ has given directions to follow (rather than leaving him to his own ingenuity or feelings) that will uphold him in the trial.

So, then, **Christ is Lord**—the **Lord** of trial! Therefore, if fear dominates, if he becomes so upset in trial that he cannot carry on successfully, something is wrong with his submission to Christ **as Lord.**

The verse speaks of **sanctifying Christ as Lord *in* the heart.** This is an important qualification. It does no good to outwardly make such an affirmation when inwardly there is doubt and unbelief. To **sanctify Christ** in the **heart** is to do so genuinely or truly. The **heart** in the Scriptures is not contrasted with the head (as in our culture)

---

5. For a development of the love/fear dynamic and for information on other aspects of the fear problem see my pamphlet, *What Do You Do When Fear Overcomes You?*

but with the lips or mouth. Peter is saying, "Don't just tell us this; mean it!"

One thing that could be wrong when **fear** prevails is a basic failure in understanding and knowledge. If a Christian doesn't know his faith adequately, he may not be able to **give a good defense of the hope within** him. The believer must be **ready** to reply, prepared at at all times, in any circumstance, to respond to persecutors or simple inquirers. He must be able to give **reasons for his expectations (hope).**

The word **defense** (*apologia*) comes from the practice in Athens, where every citizen had to be able to defend himself *personally* if he were brought to trial. There were no lawyers yet! Peter says, "If you are put on trial for your faith (literally or otherwise), **be ready** to state your case clearly and convincingly." He didn't require a carefully reasoned argument from each person (though, for some, that would be imperative), but (at the very least) a well-thought-through response that goes to the heart of the issue. At least, he should be grounded in the understanding of O.T. prophecies and their fulfillment in Christ; he ought to be able to articulate the gospel plainly, and he must be able to give a personal witness about the effects of the gospel in his own life.

However, that witness had to be coupled with **a good conscience** that grows out of **good behavior.** Otherwise, his words would be negated by his life. The spoken **defense,** then, must be backed up by the demonstration of its reality. And that all begins with the *manner* in which the **defense** is given: to be God-pleasing, it must be made in **gentleness** and **respect.**

What is meant by **gentleness** and **respect?** In the defense of the faith the believer should avoid both *contention* and *contempt*. Contention is arguing for the sake of arguing; to prove one's self correct; creating unnecessary antagonism and strife. Contempt for the person addressed almost always comes through and repels rather than attracts. Rather, the **defense** must be both kindly and concerned. The believer must show love.

The word **conscience** means (literally) "to know with" and speaks of human capability for self-knowledge and self-evaluation. A *good*

conscience is one that approves (rather than condemns) one's own attitudes and actions. Such a **conscience** leads to confidence and boldness. Clearly, the only way to have a **good conscience** is to maintain **good behavior** (i.e., **behavior** that accords with scriptural requirements; **behavior** that God also approves). When a believer lives like that, he puts the lie to **slander,** and, in the persecutor's **conscience,** puts him to shame.

Why does such unjust suffering occur? Never by chance; not because **God** has lost control of things. **God** is behind the trial and in the trial, working out His **plans.** Nothing can happen but what He has **determined.** His reasons, however, are not all immediately apparent. But if we lay hold on this fact, we can bear up under unjust suffering—it isn't useless, meaningless, absurd, as the existentialists say! Indeed, we can even get excited about the trials we face; we know that God is at work! God is up to something, and if we will, we can discover what He is up to (in part) and get involved in it ourselves.[6] So, then, it is clearly **better to suffer for doing good . . . than to suffer for doing evil.**

Introduction: Do you know what to do when unjust suffering comes? How do you respond to it? Since you can't avoid it if you're living for Christ, you'd better learn now.

    I. YOU MUST DO GOOD.
        A. This isn't new advice, but here's a new angle—
        B. Doing good will help you avoid much trouble.
        C. Yet, you may still suffer unjustly
        D. Since some hate good and try to stamp it out
        E. As they did with Christ.
   II. YOU SHOULD RESPOND PROPERLY.
        A. Don't fear or be upset.
        B. But be peaceful. How?

---

6. Cf. Paul's response to trouble—imprisonment in Rome—in Philippians 1:12-18.

C. By truly sanctifying Christ as Lord,
D. Ready to defend your hope
E. In gentleness and respect,
F. From a good conscience
G. Growing out of good behavior
H. That backs up your spoken defense
I. And puts persecutors to shame.
III. YOU SHOULD SEE GOD AT WORK.
A. Suffering for good is neither absurd nor meaningless
B. And circumstances do not seem out of God's control
C. When you recognize that suffering is a part of God's plan
D. In which He is accomplishing His purposes.
E. Then you can get involved in His program and
F. Discover that it *is* better to suffer for good than for evil
G. Both here, and hereafter.

Conclusion: Recognize the importance of what Peter has said and when unjust suffering comes for doing good, (1) continue to do good; (2) respond with a good witness for Christ; and (3) joyfully join God at work in the trial.

Section Nineteen

Christ also died for sins fully and finally, a righteous One on behalf of unrighteous ones, that He might lead you to God, being put to death in the flesh but made alive by the Spirit, by Whom also He went and preached to the spirits who are in prison because they disobeyed His Word at that time when God's patience was waiting in the days of Noah, while he was building an ark in which a few persons (eight, to be exact) were saved by water. And as a counterpart to the water, baptism now saves you (not by the removal of grime from the flesh, but by the approval of a good conscience before God through inquiry) by the resurrection of Christ, Who has gone into heaven and is at the right hand of God, over angels, and authorities, and powers who have been made subject to Him (I Pet. 3:18-22).

Peter now supports his contentions about **suffering** by referring to **Christ's** sufferings, but almost immediately moves to a discussion of the death of Christ in relationship to those who are **disobedient** to the gospel, citing (as an example) the pre-flood population that failed to heed **Noah's preaching** and (as a consequence) ended up in God's **prison.** What Peter wrote has perplexed many. I shall try to bring some understanding out of this chaos.

First, let's get the contextual relevance of this section clear. Peter wants to show the advantages of **suffering** for **doing good** *in contrast to* **suffering** for **doing evil** (vs. 17). The advantages, according to the example cited, are not merely temporal, but are also eternal. Those who **disobey** (pay no attention to, and thus reject) the gospel in the end are ruined (e.g., the destruction of the flood and eternal punishment in hell). Those who **suffer** as Christians, however like **Christ**

113

(Whose resurrection led Him in triumph over every enemy) will be (and are already in Christ) raised victoriously over all of their enemies, as (also in Him) they are **led to God.**

It is not necessary to enlarge upon the fact of the sacrificial **death of Christ for** (lit., "concerning") **sins,** which Peter reaffirms in verse 18, except to note these new points:

> (1) His death was *hapax* (i.e., "once for all" = **full and final;** cf. Heb. 9:28, etc.).
>
> (2) It was substitutionary (always implied before; here plainly stated): **a righteous One on behalf of** (*huper*) **unrighteous ones.**

The word **also** in verse 18 refers to the fact that Christ also **suffered** unjustly (relating back to verse 17), that in His case it was **also** true that this was **better** and that because it was according to **God's plan,** His purposes were furthered by Christ's suffering. The purpose noted is to bring **(lead)** Christians to God. It is precisely this that is demonstrated so vividly in Noah's experience (as we shall see).

Christ was put to death in the flesh. That is to say, His death was a truly physical one; He was genuinely human. That means He had a human body in which He **died.** But He was **made alive by the Spirit** (not *in* the spirit). That the Holy Spirit (not Christ's human spirit) in view is clear from the next verse. It was **by this Spirit** (rather than in the flesh) that, long ago in Noah's time, **He went and preached** to those who are *now* disembodied **spirits** (cf. usage in Heb. 12:23) locked up **in prison** (not merely kept in detention) as punishment.[7] **Made alive by the Spirit** refers to Christ's resurrection (cf. II Cor. 15:4; and for our resurrection in Him, I Cor. 15:22).

It was **by** the same Holy **Spirit** that **He went and preached** (cf. 4:6). Just as Paul can say in Ephesians 2:17 that Christ **preached** (after His resurrection and ascension) through the apostles, so too can Peter say that **He preached by the Spirit** to the antediluvian world **by the Spirit** through **Noah.**[8]

---

7. Tartarus, or the place of torment in the Unseen World (Hades); cf. II Peter 2:4 (these are *gloomy* pits).

8. Note that in II Peter 2:15 he calls Noah a "preacher of righteousness."

In verse 20, Peter tells us why these disembodied spirits are now being punished by **imprisonment: it is because they disobeyed** God's **word at that time when God's patience was waiting in the days of Noah, while he was building an ark.** During the 120 years prior to the flood, God's Spirit was at work with men (Gen. 6:3), presumably through Noah's **preaching.** God's **patience** is great; He waited 120 years, during which **Noah** also **was building** the **ark** (this means a box-like container). In God's providence, He achieves much at once. Through this **ark eight persons** (lit., "souls")[9] **were saved by water.**

It is altogether important to note that it was the **water** *by* **which** (not *from* which) **they were saved.** The same **water** that destroyed others lifted the **eight persons** who were in the **ark** above the destruction.

To this salvation **by water** Peter says **baptism** corresponds (**baptism** is a **counterpart,** or antitype to the **water;** i.e., the two have a strong resemblance in some respect). In what does this likeness consist?

Before answering that question, note the qualifying material in verse 21 that breaks the argument. Peter inserts this to clarify his meaning; many have only used it to further confound. Lest anybody think that he was referring to an outward ritual (*water* **baptism**) (the use of the word **water** when speaking of the flood followed by a reference to **baptism** could easily be misconstrued in this way), Peter makes it clear to everyone that he isn't talking about anything outward or physical at all.

He says, "It isn't the **water** that **removes grime from the skin** that I'm concerned about. I am speaking of an inner change that brings about a **good conscience** (one freed from the guilt of sin) because it has **approval after inquiry.** And this has been done in **God's presence.**

The **baptism** that **saves** is (of course) Spirit **baptism.** With Peter, Christians must believe in regeneration by the Spirit; not in baptismal regeneration by water. Baptismal regeneration confuses, rather

---

9. *Souls* is used in contrast to spirits (vs. 19). The spirit is the disembodied person; the soul is the person in union with the body.

than distinguishes, Spirit **baptism** with water **baptism.** Peter here makes a clear distinction between the two.

What does all this mean? In order to understand Peter's argument, omit the parenthetical material in verse 21 when reading:

. . . baptism now saves you . . . by the resurrection of Christ.

But how does **baptism** save? **By the resurrection of Christ,** Peter says. Spirit **baptism** puts a person "into Christ" (I Cor. 12:13). The argument in Romans 6 helps clarify Peter's use (I Peter seems in many ways to parallel Romans). Paul says there that we were "baptized into Christ Jesus" (vs. 3). That is, we were "baptized into every aspect of His life. He argues if we have the whole, then we have the parts; if we are in *Christ,* then we are in His circumcision, death, burial, resurrection, ascension and seating at God's right hand. His point in Romans 6 is that we must live a new life. If we are baptized into Christ, we are baptized into His death and resurrection to new life. In Colossians 2:11, 12, Paul can also say that we have been circumcised with Christ by virtue of our Spirit baptism into Him. And, in Ephesians 2:6 (see also Col. 3:1), He considers us in the heavens seated at God's right hand in Him.

Now, in verses 21, 22, Peter's point is this: Spirit **baptism saves** us **by Christ's resurrection,** *just as water saved* the eight who were in the ark. By entering into Christ through Spirit **baptism** we too can be considered raised **above angels, authorities and powers** in the **resurrection** that lifts us (in Him) above them all. Noah's experience is the type of this—the **water saved** them by buoying them above all the opposing forces that drowned in the flood. Peter argues, "There is no need, therefore, to think of those who oppose and persecute you as victors; in Christ, you have been saved from all power and influence that they could exert over you. This happened in His resurrection, by which you have been raised to a new life" (note the similarity of 4:1 to Romans 6). You were raised and you have ascended with Him and in Him.

Introduction: Suffering for doing good is better than suffering for doing evil. Do you believe that? A clear example of this is found in Christ's suffering, which (also) indicates how Christ saves you from your enemies.

I. CHRISTIAN, CHRIST DIED FOR YOU
   A. Fully and finally
   B. As a Substitute
   C. In order to lead you to God.

II. CHRIST'S RESURRECTION SAVES YOU
   A. As the waters saved the eight in the ark
   B. By buoying them up to safety.
   C. So you are lifted above all your persecutors
   D. By Spirit baptism
   E. That introduces you into Christ
   F. And the benefits of His resurrection.

III. UNBELIEVERS WERE PUNISHED
   A. By destruction in the flood
   B. And imprisonment in hell
   C. Because they rejected Christ's message
   D. That He preached by the Spirit
   E. Through Noah
   F. During God's patient waiting
   G. As he was building the ark.

Conclusion: Take heart! You are safe in Christ; as Noah was in the ark.

CHAPTER FOUR

Section Twenty

Therefore, since Christ has suffered in the flesh, arm yourselves also with that thought, because whoever has suffered in the flesh has come to a parting of the ways with sin. As a result, it is now possible to live the remainder of your time in the flesh no longer following human desires, but following God's will. (You have spent enough time in the past furthering the Gentiles' purposes, living for licentiousness, lust, drunkenness, wild partying, drinking bouts, and forbidden idolatries.) But when you do so, it surprises others that you won't run with them in the same ruinous excesses, and they insult you. But they will have to give an account to the One Who is ready to judge the living and the dead. Now this is the reason why the good news was announced to the dead that (on the one hand) they might be judged in the flesh like man, but (on the other) that they might live like God in the spirit (I Pet. 4:1-6).

This is probably the most difficult section of I Peter to interpret. Clarifying the previous section, however, does throw light on it. The basic solution to the problem of understanding verse 1 (is it talking about martyrdom or some other sort of death?) lies in a recognition of the fact that an artificial chapter division arbitrarily has been inserted here, breaking the continuity of the reader's thought. The **therefore,** with which 4:1 begins, points to the inter-relationship of the two sections. What Peter is about to say now (in some way) must grow out of what he has just been saying in chapter 3; it is quite wrong to see him abruptly taking up a new subject. There is, indeed, a smooth transition from previous material to this new section. To understand this is to grasp the key to verses 1-6.

But what has Peter been discussing (see comments on the previous section for more details)? We saw that he was talking about Spirit **baptism.** Like Paul, Peter saw the believer introduced into Christ (the word *baptizo* means to put things together, to join; *bapto* means to dip[1]) by Spirit baptism. This union with Christ by **baptism** (I Cor. 12:13; Gal. 3:27) leads to an identification of the believer with Christ (Rom. 6; Col. 2) that allows one to attribute to him all of the life, works and ministry of Christ (circumcised with Christ, crucified with Christ, buried with Christ, risen with Christ, seated in the heavenlies with Christ). Because the believer is "in Christ" (or "with Christ")—to use Paul's terminology—wherever Christ went and whatever Christ did can be said of the believer too. This is accomplished for him by the **baptism** of the Spirit. That same idea is set forth by Peter in his own distinctive terminology. As Peter notes, we have been **resurrected** with Christ, **Who has gone into heaven and is at the right hand of God. . . .** We too have done so in Him. Speaking like Paul in Romans 6 (Col. 2), in chapter 4 Peter points to the fact of this resurrection as the basis for living a new life. If we have been identified with Christ by **baptism,** and **Christ has suffered** (died) **in the flesh,** so have we. **Arming ourselves with that thought** can help us to **part ways with sin** and strike out on new paths of righteousness for His Name's sake.

Here, Peter continues the thought begun in 3:18 (Christ **suffered and died for sins fully and finally . . . being put to death in the flesh**) that was interrupted by illustrational and explanatory material (vss. 19-22). Picking up the thread again, he says Christ's death means that He is done with sin (never again must He bear them to a cross and die for them). So too, he continues, you who have died (in Christ) **have come to a parting of the ways with sin** (conversion is a fork in the road, a crossroads, where we take a new direction in Christ). That is the message of verse 1.

The old person has been put off and the new person has been put

---

1. See my book, *The Meaning and Mode of Baptism.* Surely when we are baptized "into Christ," we are not put into Him *and then removed!*

on (cf. Eph. 4; Col. 3). And, again with Paul, Peter proceeds to affirm that *in daily living* (in our experience), not only in the heavenly reckoning, we must become what we (already) are (in Christ). That is the thrust of verses 2-6 (esp. vss. 2, 3).

A word more should be said about Peter's figure of speech. His command, "arm yourselves also with that thought," is quite instructive. It indicates:

(1) that there will be battles to be fought in the parting of the ways with sin, and that

(2) thoughts—biblical thinking—can be used as weapons in those battles. God's empire is promoted by the sword of the Spirit (cf. Rev. 19:5).

In returning to the theme of 3:18, Peter now draws the implications of Christ's death **in the flesh** and applies them to the problem raised in 3:14, 17. **Suffering for righteousness** is not easy to withstand. The strongest defensive weapons must be employed. Nor must the Christian soldier be merely passive; he must "fight the good fight" and "conquer evil with **good.**" But what is it that motivates, sustains, protects? What is it that **arms** him for the battle? What can withstand the fiery darts of doubt and keep resentment from overwhelming him? Peter's answer—the **armor** and weapons of redemptive truth! Christ went through it all successfully (and you have too—in Him!). Now in the actual encounter with evil you can **follow in His steps,** and—indeed—in your own steps (in Him)! This is not new; it has happened before—it can happen again. **Arm yourself with that thought,** Christian, as you meet the foe!

Since new life in Christ means death to the old life (old person, old ways, patterns, habits, thoughts about suffering and death), **you can part ways with sin.** It is **possible.** You are no longer bound by evil to do its bidding. Christ has freed you; He is your new Master. He now rules you and commands you to **part ways with** sin's grasp, authority and power (that is the negative; the put off) and to **follow God's will** instead (that is the positive side; the put on that replaces what must be put off).

Even under the most severe trials (remember Christ's **suffering**), Peter says, the believer need not sin. He does not say this victory over the temptations brought by persecution and trial will be easy, but he does say it is **possible.** For the rest **(remainder)** of **his time in the flesh** (the rest of his life) the believer must live according to **(follow) God's will** rather than his own **desires.** This theme—following **God's** commandments rather than **desires** and feelings—permeates I Peter, and since I have already commented on it before (see comments especially on 1:14; 2:11), I shall not do so here. Simply note here that Peter makes it clear that there are no acceptable excuses for sin in **suffering** because it is Christ's very redemptive work in suffering that

(1) makes it **possible** to **part ways with sin** and resist it and
(2) sets the example for us to do so!

When the pressure is severe, it is not necessary to revert to pagan responses (following one's own **desires** and wishes). It is possible (instead) to live as **God** directs. While we **live in the flesh,** we need no longer follow the flesh. Christ has opened the **possibility** for entirely new responses.

But not only is such change in living **possible;** it is also high time for it to begin to take place! We **have** (as Peter pointedly observes) **spent enough time in the past furthering the purposes of the Gentiles** (i.e., of the unsaved, pagans). We have served sin far too long— indeed, one day, one hour, one second in sin's service is too long! But it has been more than that. All such **time** has been wasted and lost. Actually, that time was not only wasted—it was spent in harmful activity because it **furthered the purposes of the Gentiles** (i.e., it propagated paganism—its ways, thinking, etc.). As a matter of fact, we should see, such living opposed God's **purposes:** whoever doesn't "gather" (work positively to promote Christ's **purposes**) "scatters" (works negatively in opposition to them). Whether we knew it or not, that is how we have been living (cf. Rom. 5:10).

Many people don't see this. Therefore, Peter, by some obvious examples (he makes it clear by these examples that no one could mistake, but doesn't exclude less flambouyant sins), illustrates what he means.

All of the following activities listed are representative of (and in-and-of-themselves plainly demonstrate) the destructive, ruinous effects of sinful living that sour and pervert human life and spread like cancer among pagans. Here is Peter's list:

1. **Licentiousness**—Includes any and every sort of public indecency. Often it refers to outward sexual immorality of a shocking sort (cf. II Pet 2:7).

2. **Lust**—The word is usually translated **"desire."** Here it refers to all the desires, wishes and feelings (all these words in Peter's list are in the plural, denoting the frequent, repetitive nature of these offenses and the fact that they took various forms) *as they have been pursued to satisfaction.* It is not the **desire** alone that is in view (as in vs. 2), but the **desire** fulfilled.

3. **Drunkenness**—Here it is either the habitual drunkard's lifestyle or the whole complex of sinful activities that often accompany a period of drunkenness (or both) that is in view.

4. **Wild partying**—These revels could be public or private, secular or religious. The word originally signified "festal gatherings." But because such activities so often were pursued at these gatherings (cf. the Mardi Gras), it came to refer to these rather than to the gathering itself.

5. **Drinking bouts**—Drinking parties—where the *intention* was to indulge in such activities—were common then, as they are now. These usually ended in a drunken orgy.

6. **Forbidden idolatries**—These were abominable acts carried out in connection with pagan religious rites and ceremonies.

The sinful **purposes of pagans** are **furthered** when Christians participate in such activities. But the thrilling truth (attested to by Paul as well in I Cor. 9:6-11) is that when Christ sets a person free from sin, it is possible for him to abandon such a lifestyle and to **follow God's will** instead (note again the put off/put on dynamic of vs. 2).

When a Christian refuses to participate in such things, however, this may lead to trouble. When he **follows God's will,** he will no longer **run** with the crowd. In fact, as verse 4 suggests, he must even reject encouragements and refuse invitations to do so. At times the pressure others exert can be strong. Others will be **surprised** at his refusal (but the Christian should not be **surprised** at this). For them his refusal will be an *unpleasant* **surprise,** and in any number of ways they will let him know it (**insults** can take many forms—why not sketch four or five possible reactions such a refusal might elicit?).

Why do pagans **insult** Christians for their refusal to **run** with them? Because they know that these **excesses** in which they indulge are **ruinous,** yet (unlike Christians) they have no incentive or power to abandon them. Moreover, the refusal casts a reflection on their behavior. It is, in effect, a judgment against them. So it is from envy and anger at the judgment (inferred, if not actually implied) that these insults come.

But the Christian is not really their judge; Christ is (vs. 5). And, indeed, He is **ready** (nothing hinders Him; He has no hesitation about judging) to judge both **those who are alive** now and **those who have died.** And, although pagans may now seem to have the upper hand, and although they seem to be having all the good times while Christians suffer—their wild partying and sinful indulgences all seem so glamorous at the moment—the day will come when they will be called to **account.** Those who danced must pay the fiddler!

But, Peter makes clear, it isn't only his readers who have heard the **Good News;** dead believers (those who have died as martyrs may especially be in view) in the resurrection will also pass muster at the **judgment.** Though they were **judged** (condemned) **in the flesh** (by unbelievers) **like man** (i.e., according to human standards; cf. Selwyn on the plural here) they now **live** (with Christ) **like God** (a holy, perfect spirit life; cf. 1:15, 16; Heb. 12:23, in harmony with *His standards*). They didn't enter into the fullness of this **life** while they remained **in the flesh,** but now—**in the spirit**—martyrdom has led to a life like God's (cf. Rev. 20:4; II Tim. 2:11). They now live and reign with Christ.

How may these truths be preached? The thrust of the passage is that it is **possible** to endure **suffering** as **Christ** did (no excuses are allowed), living according to **God's will** (found in Scripture, of course) regardless of **pagan insults** over your refusal to indulge in sinful practices. Temptations can be thwarted by **arming** your mind with these truths, knowing that, at length, God will turn the tables (cf. II Thess. 1). The following sketch (remember, these outlines are only sketches that need filling out) may help:

Introduction: Suffering can lead to doubt and despair if you let it. You have noticed how some (perhaps yourself) cave in when pressure, trouble and temptations come. Yet others seem to endure well and even grow under trial. What makes the difference?

I. YOU MUST BE PROPERLY ARMED TO MEET TRIAL
    A. When temptation to doubt and despair attacks
    B. You need biblical armor (thinking)
    C. To withstand it
    D. And to defeat it
    E. Or you will revert to pagan responses
    F. And lose the battle with evil.

II. YOU MUST ARM YOURSELF
    A. With the thought that as Christ suffered (died),
    B. And thus came to a parting of the ways with sin,
    C. So can you
    D. Because you suffered with Him,
    E. Have died to sin with Him
    F. And have risen to new life with Him.

III. YOU ALSO MUST RECOGNIZE YOUR NEW POTENTIAL
    A. In Christ—
    B. To resist the tug of human desires
    C. And instead to be able to follow God's will
    D. Rather than ruinous pagan excesses.

IV. BUT YOU ALSO MUST REALIZE
   A. That pagans will not appreciate your refusal
   B. To run in their ways with them
   C. And will insult you.
   D. However, Christ will judge them
   E. As they have judged your dead brothers
   F. Who have entered into fullness of life
   G. Through martyrdom.

Conclusion: Recognize your conversion potential. Think and act biblically; you can—so there is no excuse for doing otherwise.

Section Twenty-one

The end of all things is near; therefore, be sound-minded and level-headed, given to prayer. Above all, love each other extensively because love covers a multitude of sins. Be hospitable to one another without grumbling. As each has received a gift, he should use it in serving the rest of you, so that you might be good stewards of God's variegated grace. When someone speaks, let him speak God's messages; when someone serves, let him serve by the strength that God supplies, so that in everything God may be glorified through Jesus Christ, to Whom be glory and might forever and ever. Amen (I Pet. 4:7-11).

Peter has spoken of the **judgment** of unbelievers who are persecuting his readers by **judging** them according to pagan (human) standards (**like man**). This state of affairs will not continue. Its **end** is at the door. Peter reveals this to encourage his readers to persevere in trial. There will be a termination of the present persecution.

I Peter was written before A.D. 70 (when the destruction of Jerusalem took place); Selwyn is probably correct in arguing for an A.D. 63/64 date of composition. The persecution (and martyrdom) that these (largely) Jewish Christians had been experiencing up until now stemmed principally from unconverted Jews (indeed, his readers had found refuge among **Gentiles** as resident aliens. It is true (as vs. 4 indicates) that the **Gentiles** had begun to **insult** and slander them (see earlier chapters on this), but this was only the beginning of a new persecution of a different sort about which Peter will have more to say in the next session (vss. 12ff.). Here, he refers to the severe trials that came upon Christians who had fled Palestine under attack from their unconverted fellow Jews. **The end of all things** (that had brought this exile about) was **near.**

In six or seven years from the time of writing, the overthrow of Jerusalem, with all its tragic stories, as foretold in the book of Revelation and in the Olivet Discourse upon which that part is based, would take place. Titus and Vespasian would wipe out the old order once and for all. **All** those forces that led to the persecution and exile of these Christians in Asia Minor—the temple ceremonies (outdated by Christ's death), Pharisaism (with its distortion of O.T. law into a system of works-righteousness) and the political stance of Palestinian Jewry toward Rome—would be erased. The Roman armies would wipe Jewish opposition from the face of the land. Those who survived the holocaust of A.D. 70 would themselves be dispersed around the Mediterranean world. "So," says Peter, "hold on; **the end is near.**"[2] The full **end** of the O.T. order (already made defunct by the cross and the empty tomb) was about to occur.

Based on this additional encouragement, Peter urges calm, sane living upon his readers. There is no reason to push the panic button; there is going to be "a way of escape" soon (I Cor. 10:13). "But in the meanwhile," he says, "here is what you must do":

(1) **Be sound-minded and level-headed.** That is, keep cool under pressure. Don't allow emotion to take over. **Follow God's will,** not your feelings, when the going gets tough. The ideas of balanced thinking and living, along with calmness and self-control are inherent in this command. There is no cause for alarm; so they must not act out of alarm. All is in God's hands, proceeding on course according to His timetable. And, the hour for the cessation of the present persecution is at hand. Since relief is so close—just around the next corner—don't blow it now by going off half-cocked. Instead, maintain decorum, and live in a steady, calm way, doing good. **Prayer** will sustain you and enable you to do so (cf. Matt. 26:41).

---

2. Obviously Peter could not be referring to the **end** of the New Testament era because (as a prophet) he knew that it was *not* **near** (cf. II Pet. 3:1-13; for more on eschatology see my book, *The Time Is at Hand*).

(2) **Above all, love each other extensively.** It is of prime importance to show love toward one another. During the interim, while this pressure continues, mutual **love** among the brothers and sisters will help each individual to maintain and manifest his faith. "You **love** one another already, of course," Peter says (in effect), "but I'm calling for love that reaches further; that **extends** beyond anything you have known before." **Love** ought to **extend** to every need in every person. Such **love** will encourage all. But it will also ease your personal relationships and cement you more closely together (elsewhere, **love** is called a "bond"; Col. 3:14), because as your **love** extends it will seek to **cover** more and more **sins.** This **love** will cause you to overlook a great number of **sins** against you. As your love abounds, it will **cover** offenses so that they are not allowed to come between you and others. Fightings, grudges and bad feelings among the brothers in time of persecution is especially tragic; it could destroy much—don't let it. That is the message. "Be very cautious therefore" (Peter is saying in these words) "that your **love** for one another **extends** even to the point of **covering** each other's **sins** (**covering sins** means not allowing them to come between you and another). **Covering sins** is not a call for holding grudges and building resentments, but for the very opposite. One must overlook and forgive. Cf. Proverbs 10:12.

(3) **Hospitality** must be extended and maintained **without grumbling.** This was particularly important for the spread of the Christian faith. Travelling missionaries depended upon **hospitality** for lodging and food and travel expenses. That was one reason why Diotrophes' offense was so serious (cf. III John). **Hospitality** was to be offered freely, cheerfully, in love and out of concern; there was to be no complaining or **grumbling.** Those who fail to offer **hospitality** freely miss the blessings that it brings. This reference to **hospitality** does not exclude local **hospitality**; indeed, that seems to be para-

mount in Peter's thinking (note the words **to one another;** this could refer to Christians in general but probably refers to others in the Christian community to which Peter writes). Perhaps, among other things, Peter has in mind opening one's home to meetings of the local church. If so, that makes a very natural transition into verses 10, 11.

(4) **Gifts** (of hospitality, or those that follow) **must be used to serve the rest.** No one has exclusive rights to the gifts God has entrusted to him. They were given *not to him but to the church* (cf. Eph. 4), and they were intended to be **used in the service** of the whole church, for its benefit (cf. I Cor. 12:7, 14-31). The modern idea—so prevalent in some quarters—of the personal orientation of **gifts** (they were given to *me;* for *my* benefit) is *entirely* wrong. They are **gifts** not to individuals but to the church as a whole. This is made clear not only from their intended **use** (**to serve the rest**) but also from the fact that each Christian is considered not to be an owner or possessor of a **gift** but a **steward** of it. Thus, he must so share the **variegated grace of God** in which he has participated, that he helps to bring unity out of diversity. Any preacher or counselor who fails to stress the **stewardship** of **gifts,** asking how well it has been kept, misses a key point in the passage.

(5) **Gifts** must be used humbly to **glorify God.** Peter refers to the use of two **gifts** that characterize (and thereby identify) each of the two offices in the church: **speaking** and **serving** (not that these are mutually exclusive). When functioning in these offices, a Christian must do so humbly; not pushing himself forward or taking **glory** for himself. He must give **glory to God** by recognizing that all he does comes from God's grace. Preaching elders really have nothing to **speak** about unless they **speak God's messages.** Deacons could never **serve** properly in their temporal practical ministries unless God **supplied** (lit., choreographed) **the strength to do so.** When officers recognize this and **in the use of their**

gifts give God the honor due Him, God will receive **glory in everything.** The words **in everything** show that nothing we do or are comes from ourselves; all is of grace.

In this doxology the great goal of all human service stands out clearly: **glorify God in everything.** God is glorified in His Son **Jesus Christ,** Who redeemed us. To the Father and Son, and to the Spirit Who strengthens, belong **glory and might forever.** The **Amen** fulfills the role of adding emphasis to this great truth. It is stronger than an exclamation point; it means, "May it really be so!"

Now, for the sketch that unifies this section. (Actually, the section alone would make an excellent five-sermon series with each of the five points developed fully.)

Introduction: There are times when it looks like trouble will never end. That is probably the point just before it does! Peter told his readers exactly that. "But," someone asks, "what do you do in the interim, while you are waiting for the end?" That is a good question, to which Peter addresses himself in these verses.
In times of persecution . . .

I. YOU MUST KEEP YOUR HEAD IN TRIAL
    A. Be sound-minded and level-headed
    B. Rather than following feeling
    C. When the going gets rough;
    D. God is in control and all is happening on schedule.
    E. Don't blow it when relief is at the door;
    F. Keep your head cool by praying.

II. YOU MUST LOVE ONE ANOTHER
    A. As a top priority item
    B. You must show mutual love
    C. That extends as far as possible
    D. And covers a multitude of sins.

III. YOU MUST MAINTAIN HOSPITALITY
    A. For Christian teachers,

B. In normal social relations with Christian friends
C. And in housing Christian meetings;
D. But you must do it cheerfully
E. Without grumbling.

IV. YOU MUST USE YOUR GIFTS
A. To serve the whole body
B. As good stewards of God's trust,
C. Not selfishly possessing them for yourself,
D. So that all may benefit
E. And the diversity of gifts
F. Will bring about true unity.

V. YOU MUST DEMONSTRATE HUMILITY
A. In your use of gifts
B. Elders recognizing that they speak God's messages,
C. Deacons declaring that they minister out of God's resources,
D. Thus giving all the glory to God
E. Whose glory and might deserve to be extolled forever
F. In everything!

Conclusion: What activity! Surely trial is a time for concerted effort, not the time for inactivity. There is more than enough to keep you busy serving Christ and to keep your eyes off your own misfortunes.

Section Twenty-two

Dear friends, don't be surprised at the fiery ordeal that is coming upon you to test you, as though something strange were happening to you; rather, insofar as you share in Christ's sufferings, be glad, that at the revelation of His glory you may be very glad. If you are reproached because of Christ's name, you are happy, because the Spirit of glory and of God rests on you. Now, let none of you suffer because he is a murderer, or thief, or criminal or even as a meddler, but if anybody suffers because he is a Christian, let him not be ashamed, but let him glorify God in that Name. I say this because it is time for judgment to begin with God's household; and if it starts with us, how will it end with those who disobey God's good news? And, "if the righteous man is scarcely saved, where will the ungodly and sinner appear?" So then, let those who suffer according to God's will do good and entrust themselves to a faithful Creator (I Pet. 4: 12-19).

Peter has just spoken about God's **glory** in the preceding verses that extol Him in a magnificent doxology. He now continues the theme, developing the concept of **glory,** coming back to it time and again. Peter was struck with the **glory** that he had witnessed in the transfigured Christ on the mountain, and could never get away from it. He looked forward to the day when Christ's full **glory** would once again be revealed—this time—to all men, and to the fact that even *now* Christians could **glorify** Him (extol Him as the glorious One) by their behavior and words. He also understood how believers would share in that eternal **glory,** and how—even in this life—as faithful martyrs and confessors, they could begin to enter into it already. Peter is excited about the **glory** of Christ!

Peter also has spoken of the cessation of Jewish persecution and about the relief (temporary though it may be) that this would afford (vs. 7). Now, in what follows, it is his task to predict a second wave of persecution, a second **ordeal,** more **fiery** than the first: the Roman (Neronian) persecution of the church. But he makes no apologies for this. To the contrary, he speaks (as we see) of **glory: glory** to God and to His people coming out of it. Pastors, and Christian workers, must never apologize to new converts when they warn them (and they must do so!) of the trials of their new-found Christian life. Rather, with Peter, they should point them to the joys and **glory** of **sharing Christ's sufferings** and bearing His **Name.**

The Jewish persecution would abate with the destruction of Jerusalem (cf. notes on the previous section). But a persecution, worse than the first, soon would overtake them. They must be ready for it. The relief would be welcome, but it must be considered only a breathing space. There would be no possibility of settling back. The Jewish persecution would be but preparation for the Roman. Now the real **test** would **come upon** them! Peter reveals this beforehand so that when it comes they will not be taken by **surprise.** He would not have them asleep. He did not want them to think of it as **something strange;** they should be fully acquainted with the facts.

Nor should it seem **strange** from another angle—persecution is nothing more or less than **sharing in the sufferings of Christ.** Not that Christians could (or would ever need to) enter into Christ's redemptive work—that surely isn't Peter's point! But as a part of His body, there were many things they would **suffer** because the world hates Him. And, since they would bear His **Name** (as Peter will observe in vs. 16), their close identification with Him would bring trouble to them.

Suffering itself doesn't bring happiness; but Peter says **be glad.** Why? Not **glad** that you are **suffering,** but **glad** that you may **suffer** for Him. That joy comes from the possibility of showing Him how deeply you love Him by enduring unsought, unjust persecution for His sake. And, Peter adds, if you **gladly suffer** for Him now, at Christ's **revelation** (or unveiling) when His **glory** as God will be made known to all (cf. 1:7), you will **be very glad.** Indeed, you who have **shared** His **sufferings** now will **share** in His **glory** then! That bright prospect too will bring **gladness** to your hearts even in heartache and pain.

The **test** to which Peter alludes (vs. 12) is not really in the **fiery ordeal** itself; it is in the believer. That is where it goes on. The persecution provides not only opportunity for purification (**fiery ordeal** in the light of 1:6, 7 seems to carry something of that impact), but also a means for testing that reveals to each professed Christian how genuine and how virile his faith may be. In America, there has been no Roman persecution of the church, and the **tests** that purify and reveal are of a different nature.

In verse 14 there is surely a reference to Matthew 5:11. As **the Spirit of glory and of God** (or "even of God," or "Which is from God") **rested upon** Jesus, so too will He descend in power imparting strength and wisdom to every genuine believer who suffers, in order to

1. enable him to withstand the persecution,
2. witness a good confession before his persecutors,
3. bring **glory** to Jesus Christ by bearing His Name nobly in the **ordeal.**

Cf. Stephen's face during his trial (Acts 6:15). The **Spirit** Who filled him with grace and power (6:8) also manifested that fact to his persecutors. This same **Spirit,** Who brought **glory** to Christ then, will help believers to **glorify** Him now. So, don't *fear* the worst; in the worst God promises to send His Best!

Let me tell you, however, Peter warns, that all this applies to **suffering** for Christ's sake; it doesn't characterize all **suffering.** And it especially has nothing whatever to do with suffering that you bring on yourself by your own sinful conduct. Don't get the two things confused! Therefore, don't let any of you **suffer because he is a murderer, a thief, or criminal or even as a meddler.** All of these words are straightforward and need no further explanation. The list is not intended to be exhaustive; again Peter works with clearcut extremes (as in vs. 3, q.v.), except that here he tacks on **meddlers** at the end, presumably to make it perfectly clear that the more obvious sins (actually crimes) are not the only sort of things that he has in mind. As before, the basic list contains the obvious because that takes less argumentation or explanation.

Now, in verse 16, Peter returns to his main concern: **suffering** for **Christ's** sake. One **suffers** because he is a **Christian** (i.e., a known, baptized convert who bears the **Name**). The name **Christian** is used only here and in Acts 11:26; 26:28.

He warns against being **ashamed** of Christ. Peter knew the bitterness and sorrow that could accompany such shame. That memories of his threefold denial of Jesus prior to the crucifixion flashed back as he penned these words is nearly certain. The alternative to being **ashamed** is to **glorify God in Christ's Name.** He is **glorified**

(1) by exemplary behavior in persecution that makes it clear to all that he **suffers as a Christian** and not as a wrongdoer;

(2) by bearing witness to Jesus as the *Messiah* (i.e., declaring the truth to which the **Name Christ** (the "Anointed One") bears witness (for a fuller understanding of the term consult a good Bible dictionary as you begin the study).

All this Peter urges because he sees **judgment coming.** It is **judgment beginning with God's household** (the church). The **judgment** in view is *in this world,* and stems from the fury of unbelievers against the body bearing **Christ's** Name. But God's eternal **judgment** against these persecutors (and all **who disobey God's good news**[3]) will follow. If things seem bad now for believers (vs. 18), so bad that it seems as if hardly any will escape (**be saved**), think of what will happen to people who don't know God and whose sins have never been forgiven when God begins to **judge** them! Cf. Luke 23:31 (Prov. 11:31, LXX).

And the upshot of it all (vs. 19), as my choice of a title for this volume indicates, is that Peter tells the believer—in a great and glorious statement of how to withstand persecution—precisely what to do:

---

3. Cf. comments on 1:22.

(1) **Entrust** yourselves to **a faithful Creator** (or, possibly, as Calvin translates it, Protector). If He is the **Creator,** He can do all things, and all things are in His control. Therefore, He knows and wills what is best. So, unquestioningly put your life in His hands. Moreover, He is **faithful** (i.e., One in Whom you can place full faith); you can depend on Him. He will never let you down, never go back on His Word; He is entirely trustworthy.

(2) **Do good.** The believer never needs to suffer passively without recourse. The Scriptures always call for aggressive action in persecution by which evil may be met and defeated; cf. Rom. 12:21). For more on this very important matter, see comments on 1:13.

Introduction: Sometimes things go from bad to worse. You emerge from one difficulty only to face a more serious one. Peter had to tells his readers that this would happen to them. Notice how he tells you to handle it:

I. YOU SHOULD NOT BE SURPRISED
    A. Even at the fiery ordeal
    B. As if this test were unusual;
    C. Because God has warned you about it
    D. And told you what to do.

II. YOU SHOULD BE GLAD
    A. Not over suffering itself
    B. But over suffering for Christ;
    C. Out of love for Him,
    D. Witnessing to His Name,
    E. Sharing His sufferings,
    F. Receiving the Spirit of glory now to help you
    G. And ultimately rejoicing at His revelation
    H. Rather than suffering for your own sins.

III. YOU SHOULD KNOW
   A. That if severe judgment begins with you
   B. It will end far more severely with your persecutors,
   C. That there is a way to suffer properly:
   D. By entrusting your life to a faithful Creator
   E. And doing good!

Conclusion: Trust and Obey!

CHAPTER FIVE

CHAPTER FIVE

Section Twenty-three

Therefore I urge the elders among you, as a fellow elder and witness of Christ's sufferings and as a sharer of the glory that is going to be revealed, to shepherd God's flock among you, looking after it; not out of obligation but willingly, as God would have you do it; not out of eagerness to make a personal profit, but out of eagerness to serve; not by lording it over those allotted to your charge, but by becoming models for the flock. Then, when the chief Shepherd appears, you will receive the glorious crown that will never fade (I Pet. 5:1-4).

Because (as Peter has said at the conclusion of his remarks in the previous chapter) the church would **suffer a fiery ordeal,** and because he wanted his readers **not** to **be ashamed** of Christ when the screws were tightened, Peter now turns his attention to **the elders among** the Christian exiles in Asia Minor and urges them to carry out their offices to the full, in the proper way, for the correct motives.

These church leaders would play an important part in holding the **flock** together when the test came. Their care, or the lack of it, in many lives would make the difference. An ordered, well-trained, well-organized, well-cared-for body of sheep could withstand much. But it would take leadership that was both competent and faithful to bring this about. Now, as then, in the midst of very different sorts of problems, good leadership is every bit as essential to the welfare of **God's flock.**

An **elder** (the word signifies one who is experienced or mature in the faith) is a ruling (or ruling/teaching) leader of the church. The one unchangeable office, that continued throughout the O.T. and was perpetuated in the N.T., is the **eldership.** In O.T. times, whether there was a theocracy or a monarchy, there was an **eldership** (lit., presbytery). Whether the Jews were in the land of Palestine or in exile or in dispersion, there was an **eldership.** Whether the temple was the center of worship with its many officers or whether there was worship conducted in synagogues, there was an **eldership.** And the same office—with Christian modifications—continued right into the book of Acts and the epistles without the blinking of an eyelash, just as smoothly as possible.

The **elder** and the **bishop** (**episcopas;** in vs. 2 the verbal form of this word is used) are one and the same person, as they are in Titus 1 and Acts 20 (where the words are used interchangeably). But why are there two names for the same officer? The word **elder** speaks of the man himself and of his qualifications for the office: he must be *mature* in the faith. **Bishop** speaks of the work (**overseeing**) to which he is called. Unlike many other functions that one carries out in life, this task of leading **God's flock** is described from both sides. God is concerned both to pinpoint the *work* and the sort of *person* who ought to engage in it. Men whose *lives* accord with the criteria in Paul's letters to Timothy and to Titus and whose *knowledge* and *beliefs* are true qualify as **elders** (by their maturity in faith and life they meet the test). By commissioning such a man is given authority to **oversee**[1] **God's** church, *ruling* and *caring* for it.

Peter also held the office of **overseer** and was, therefore, an **elder.** He addresses the **elders** in the congregations of Asia Minor as **fellow elders.** By this, he appeals to the solidarity in responsibility and experience that he shares with them. He too is a shepherdly leader (cf. John 21). He has done the work they are doing, has faced the problems they face and knows the temptations that are peculiar to men who hold the office (In the next two verses, he speaks about these temptations). So, both to encourage ("Men, I'm in this with you") and to warn ("I know what your temptations are like"), Peter refers to himself as a **fellow elder.**

---

1. Overseeing is overseeing *as a shepherded.* For study on this and on shepherding in general, see my *Shepherding God's Flock,* vol. I, chap. 2; vol. III, chaps. 1 and 2.

But he goes beyond too. He has greater experience and wants them to know that he speaks from that vantage point as well: he was **an eyewitness** of Christ's sufferings (Peter chose the word **sufferings** because of its thematic value in this letter, but here it certainly takes up the entire complex of redemptive events associated with the cross —the resurrection and ascension as well as the death and burial). Peter was an apostle; apostles must have been eyewitnesses of Christ (cf. I Cor. 9:1). But there is even more. He was one of the privileged three witnesses chosen to accompany Christ on the Mount of Transfiguration, where he became **a sharer of the glory that is going to be revealed** (cf. II Pet. 1:17; I Pet. 4:13). Out of this background Peter urged: **Shepherd God's flock among you, looking after it** (vs. 2a).

The shepherdly figure of speech was a common one. God called Himself "The **Shepherd** of Israel." Jesus said that He was the good **Shepherd** (John 10), and Paul spoke about **shepherding the flock** (Acts 20). But, doubtless, Peter's use of the image goes back to John 21, where the risen Christ restored Him, using the very image.

But there are three outstanding problems in leadership that must be avoided. Peter succinctly sketches both the problem and its solution:

(1) *Servile service.* Christ wants no elder serving Him as an undershepherd out of mere obligation or sense of duty ("I took the job; I guess I'll have to live with it"). There is any number of tasks that one may have to do out of duty, but that is not the way that an **elder** can pursue the work of oversight. He may not serve **out of obligation** because he must become a **model** (as we shall see) in service as in all things. The flock should see in him an example of joyful service. He must serve **willingly, as God would have him do it.** This last clause is a very close approximation of Paul's words about cheerful giving in II Corinthians 9:7, where we are informed that "God loves a cheerful giver." To paraphrase Peter's words in Paul's phraseology, one would not be inaccurate in saying, "God loves a willing leader." Peter

now turns to the second temptation:

(2) *Desire for personal gain.* It has not been unknown for men, in all ages and places, to find ways of turning church authority into a means of receiving **personal** gain. There are some who seek out office for **personal** advantage. Many who enter the **eldership** with pure motives experience a change of motive in time. It is not wrong to make **personal profit,** per se. But it is wrong to use the eldership *as a means for obtaining it,* or to be **eager** for **personal** advantage. One's enthusiasm (**eagerness**) must grow out of the work, not out of the pay. The elder always must be enthusiastic about ministry, not money. When he loses this **eagerness,** he must stop and reexamine his motives. He may find that money has replaced ministry. But there is a third temptation:

(3) *Driving by domineering.* Stamping out the lust for power is always a problem with any successful leader, especially if his work is acclaimed by others. There is always a temptation to run roughshod over others, to expect privileges, demand concessions and (in general) to *drive* rather than *lead.* Pride and power are twin brothers. But sheep must be led. Peter asserts that

  (a) Pastors have no *personal* power or authority over **God's sheep.** The ***portion*** of the **flock** over which they rule, and which they **serve,** has been ***allotted*** to their **charge** by Another—**the Chief Shepherd** of **God's flock.** God owns the **flock;** Christ has full and absolute authority over it.

  (b) Pastors **serve** and rule only a portion of the **flock;** not the whole. Therefore, they all are on a par with one another. These many **elders** (of whom Peter was one) have the right (and obligation) to rebuke and correct one another. None is an absolute lord or ruler in any sense whatever. Christ alone holds that kind of dominion over His church.

Rather than drive, the true **shepherd** leads **the flock.**

146

He does so by becoming a **model** of what he urges on the sheep. He not only preaches tithing; he tithes. He not only teaches witnessing; he witnesses. He asks nothing of the **flock** that he is unwilling to *show* them how to do.

Peter doesn't end his discussion on the negative note of warning. Rather, he concludes with a marvelous promise of reward to those who serve well. The **Chief Shepherd** (cf. John 10; Heb. 13:20) will come to inspect His **flock** and to judge how well His undershepherds have cared for it. Those who have done well will receive **the glorious crown that will never fade.** This reward is like Christ's (cf. Heb. 2:9). Unlike earthly **crowns** (wreaths), made of parsley (or other greens), this **crown** will not dry up and turn brown; it is eternal.

Introduction: It is important not only for you elders to know what Christ expects of you, but for all the flock to know too. That's why Peter writes publicly (not in a private letter addressed to elders only). Here's what he says:
Elders . . .

I. CHRIST CALLS YOU TO SHEPHERD GOD'S FLOCK.
   A. This command to shepherd
   B. Addressed to mature men,
   C. Qualified for the work of overseeing,
   D. Takes on rich biblical connotations
   E. That speak of total care of sheep.
II. THERE ARE TEMPTATIONS YOU MUST AVOID:
   A. Servile obligation can be avoided
   B. By cultivating a willing spirit
   C. That God loves;
   D. Eagerness for personal profit can be countered

147

E. By developing enthusiasm for the work itself;
F. Domineering authoritarianism can be averted
G. By recognizing your proper position
H. And by becoming models to lead the flock.

Conclusion: God promises a glorious crown to you if you follow His directions and heed His warnings.

Section Twenty-four

Likewise, younger men, submit yourselves to your elders. All of you tie on the apron of humility toward one another, because "God opposes the proud but helps the humble." Humble yourselves, therefore, under the mighty hand of God, that at the proper season He may raise you up. Throw all your worry on Him, because your affairs matter to Him. Be level-headed and wide awake; your opponent the devil prowls around like a roaring lion searching for somebody to devour. Resist him, standing firm in the faith, knowing that your brotherhood throughout the world fully experiences the same kind of sufferings (I Pet. 5:5-9).

Peter now closes his letter. His closing words consist of a final exhortation to **humility** (vss. 5-7), a final warning about the **devil** (vss. 8, 9), a final encouragement concerning **God's help** (vss. 10, 11) and a final **greeting** (vss. 12-14).

First, the final exhortation. Speaking of the **elders** reminds Peter to address a word to the **younger men** (in vs. 5, **elder** means "older man"; the word is not used, as before, to refer to the office). If **elderly** men are to be respected, and the implication of all that Peter has written indicates this (cf. chap. 3, where **submission** involves obedience and respect), **younger men** must submit to them. Peter, however, doesn't enlarge upon this point. It is a timely word that calls for mutual cooperation among Christians of various age groups and points toward the basic way of effecting it (cf. I Tim. 4:1).

Next, Peter speaks to **all** (**elders, elderly men, younger men,** women, girls, children) about **humility.** In vivid language, he urges each one to securely fasten the knots as he **ties on** himself the slave's

149

apron of humility toward one another (cf. John 13:4ff. for the probable source of the image). **Humility** involves:

(1) Recognizing one's true place in life; neither thinking nor pretending to be more than one is. Realizing that all that is worthwhile has been given by God in grace also is significant in sobering one's evaluation of self.

(2) It is putting others' interests first (cf. Phil. 2), as Christ put the church before His own concerns in His humiliation.

Humility, as these facts show, is active, not merely a passive attitude. It is possible to **humble** oneself in obedience to a command.

The reason appended to this command is that **God opposes the proud, but helps the humble** (cf. Prov. 3:24; James 4:6). During the coming persecution, all the **help from God** that is available (and it is considerable, as vs. 10 indicates) will be needed. But **proud** persons will not receive it. It is as if God were to say about a **proud** person, "He thinks he is sufficient in himself, does he? Well, let's see how he handles persecution without My **help.**" But it is even stronger than that: God not only withholds **help,** He **opposes** the **proud** (vs. 5).

So, Peter repeats, **Humble yourselves, therefore, under God's mighty hand.** Here, one humbles himself by asking God to crush his pride beneath His powerful hand. When He does, God raises him up and exalts him with the *other* hand! (cf. Luke 18:14). This raising up doesn't always come at once; it occurs **at the proper season** (i.e., in God's good time). Part of humility is willingness to patiently wait for things according to God's timetable. These verses teach, then, that **God helps** those who *don't* help themselves!

We can **throw** off the burdens we carry onto God's shoulders. That is the wonderful fact of humility. **Proud** men go on struggling and **worrying** about them all by themselves. But all our trials are known to God. Troubles among loved ones, heartaches over the work—all these things He knows and wants us to prayerfully cast on Him. In humble reliance upon His wisdom, power and faithfulness, we can unburden our hearts. He has invited us. What relief! What hope! What joy!

He *cares* about us. He knows our concerns, no matter how personal, how small. **Our affairs matter to Him.** The very hairs of our heads are numbered. Small gods can be concerned about only great matters. Human problems are mere trivia to them. But our infinite, omniscient God is concerned even about the so-called trivia of our lives. There is no burden so inconsequential that we may not bring it to Him: **Throw *all* your worry on Him!**

Now to the second part of this section: Peter's final warning. While the **devil** plays his part in stirring up the Roman persecution of the church, this is not his only attack, nor is it necessarily the most effective one. Indeed, for some, it may be more diversionary than direct. At any rate, here (vss. 8, 9) Peter has in mind indirect attacks that are less than obvious. Notice how he puts it: **Be level-headed and wide awake.** The temptations to which he refers must be more covert than overt if one might fail to be **awake** to them. Smaller, personal struggles (dissension in the home or church, envy, sexual indiscretions, etc.) strike down more Christians than Roman swords. **Level-headed** thinking growing out of **wide-awake** awareness is essential to avoid the **devil's** more covert attacks therefore. Those who can withstand the enemy on the open field in battle may find themselves brought down by a sniper behind the lines; be awake to and think clearly about this possibility. The picture is expanded. While Christians doze, **the devil** creeps up on them. Then, **like a roaring lion,** he pounces upon them.

Well, what can be done about this? **Resist him.** How? **Resist him**

(1) by assuming an alert, **wide-awake,** thoughtful posture about the "smaller" areas of life as well as the larger ones.

(2) **by standing firm in the faith** (i.e., on the teachings of the apostles). Avoiding doubts and shaky teaching is essential. Bad doctrine opens up all sorts of territory for the devil to attack.

(3) by recognizing that your situation isn't unique: **your brotherhood throughout the world fully experiences the same kinds of sufferings.** To fail to recognize this is to open the door to self-pity and despair. To recognize that hundreds of Christians have successfully faced similar stituations in Christ

151

can lead to hope and strength. The word **brotherhood** shows the close ties that Peter wanted his readers to recognize. Christians come to false conclusions about this matter when they isolate themselves from other Christians. To recognize and maintain warm ties with other believers **throughout the world** is one way to avoid such tendencies.[2]

Note, especially, that there is nothing in the passage about rebuking the **devil** or about employing any other ritualistic form ("pleading the blood") in **resisting the devil. Resistance** grows out of strong Christian living! In James 4:7, as well as here, **resistance** is closely connected with **humble** submission to and reliance upon God. In both, **proud persons** are said to be **opposed** by God (cf. James 5:5-7). It is the **humble** person, relying on **God's help** at all points who **resists; pride** opens a Christian to **temptation** and "goes before a fall."

Thirdly, Peter writes final words of encouragement about **God's help (grace,** in these contexts, most frequently means **help).** In verse 5 Peter said that **God helps the humble.** How? Here is what **God** does for His own to enable them to **resist the devil:**

(1) **God equips** them—by His Word and Spirit with wisdom, direction and insight.

(2) **God supports**—When He is needed, He is there to call upon. He encourages through His Word and His church.

(3) **God strengthens**—We must fight; ordinarily God does not fight our battles for us. But we cannot **stand** in our own strength. God knows what we need and provides it.

(4) **God establishes**—He turns uncertainties into sureties; doubts into convictions. He confirms our faith.

All these things God does for **humble,** reliant believers. This section forms a glorious climax to the letter. Yes, you will have to **suffer for a short time,** but ultimately, Peter asserts, God will do even more. He will bring you into the fullness of **His eternal glory in Christ** (the glories of the perfected state at death). Because Peter himself is over-

---

2. A shut-in can narrow her world to four walls. Self-pity results. A counselor who helps her to read, write to and pray for missionaries around the world, can lead her out of it. Christians must have a world perspective.

whelmed by what he has written, he breaks forth into doxology.

To Him be power forever and ever. Amen!

Now, at last, comes the epilogue with its final words of **greeting.** Doubtless, this postscript was penned by Peter himself (cf. Gal. 6: 11-16 for Paul's comments on this practice). **Silvanus** (cf. II Cor. 1:9) was the amanuensis who actually wrote the bulk of Peter's letter. The warm recommendation of **Silvanus** as **a faithful brother** probably indicates that he would also bear this letter to the church of Asia Minor.

Peter sums up the general purpose of his letter, giving his main thrust. In the face of suffering and trial, he wanted to **testify to** them that their faith was **true** and to **urge** them to **stand firm in it.** It would be hard to do so at times; but they could turn again and again to this letter on such occasions and find **help.** The same is true today.

Words of greeting are conveyed from the church of Rome (**She who is at Babylon**;) cf. Revelation 14:8; 16:19; 18:2, a church consisting of fellow **chosen ones.** A personal greeting from **Mark** is passed on. Peter affectionately calls him his **son.** The **kiss** of Christian love is encouraged, and at the very end, a prayer for **peace** upon every true Christian. Peter not only expressed warm fellowship in these greetings but, like other apostles, encouraged it.

Introduction: How does a prophet close his words about suffering? With a final summary of his major emphases, not repeating, but further emphasizing them in new ways. Moreover, he adds new thrusts previously untouched. This is Peter's conclusion.

I. YOU MUST HUMBLE YOURSELVES.
   A. Young and old alike
   B. Must tie on the apron of humility
   C. Because God opposes the proud
   D. And helps the humble.
   E. You need all of His help that you can get to withstand persecution

F. And to avoid worry.
II. YOU MUST RESIST THE DEVIL
   A. By humble reliance on God,
   B. Awake to his more subtle temptations,
   C. Standing firm in the truth of the faith
   D. And recognizing that others have too.
   E. He will help you by
      equipping you
      supporting you
      strengthening you
      establishing you, and finally by
      taking

Conclusion: God's
promoting fello

by